STAYING
ALIVE!

"To cross the Pacific Ocean,
even under the most favourable circumstances,
brings you for many days close to nature,
and you realise the vastness of the sea."

from *Sailing Alone Around the World,*
by Captain Joshua Slocum (1899)

STAYING ALIVE!

117 days adrift—the incredible saga of a
courageous couple who outwitted death at sea
for a longer period than any humans before

Maurice and Maralyn Bailey

Library

owa

Foreword by Sir Peter Scott

Drawings by Peter A. G. Milne

Maps by Alan Irving

David McKay Company, Inc.
New York

LIBRARY OF CONGRESS CATALOG CARD NUMBER: 74-77039

ISBN: 0-679-50458-3

MANUFACTURED IN THE UNITED STATES OF AMERICA

Contents

List of Illustrations

Publisher's Note

Maurice and Maralyn Bailey started writing their story whilst still on board the rescue ship *Weolmi*. On their return to England, they were able to use Maralyn's diary and Maurice's log book as a 'memory bank' for the completion of their text, all of which was hand written by them.

The authors have taken immense pains to ensure that the details and chronology of their story are as near correct as possible. The drawings also have been under their close control, the artist, Peter A. G. Milne, and the cartographer, Mr. Alan Irving, having followed precisely their notes, sketches, and personal instructions.

Some of the facts stated concerning fishes and birds are to some degree at variance with established sources, but have been checked as far as was possible. Sir Peter Scott gave valuable advice concerning the marine life of the Galápagos area, with which he is familiar, and the authors' observations will be read with interest by naturalists.

Some clarification is needed concerning the diary entries and the exact number of days spent in the raft.

The numbers in circles in the diary were entered in ballpoint pen when Maralyn was aboard the rescue ship. They refer to the number of days which had passed up till 0800 on the date shown. Thus on the day marked '50', for example, the happenings entered occurred on April 23rd which was their 51st day in the raft.

Similarly, the rescue on June 30th is marked in the diary as being on day number 118, whereas it actually occurred on the 119th day. They had, therefore, spent in total 118 and a third days adrift.

To minimize confusion the shoulder notes are marked with the date followed by Maralyn's day-count in brackets.

The title of this book was kept as '117 Days Adrift' because the adventure was generally known as such from the initial news reports, though these were subsequently found to be in error.

Nautical Publishing Company, Limited
Lymington, England
October 1973

Foreword

Recently several yachts have been sunk or damaged
after collision with whales, and sometimes the crews
have felt that their boats were deliberately attacked.
After discussing this with marine biologists I cannot
find enough clear evidence to suggest a reason for such
attacks. Perhaps those in small craft who feel threatened
by whales should start an engine or bang on the hull, as
such mechanical noises might warn a whale that the
boat is not another animal, which could be a rival or a
source of food.

The survival of Maurice and Maralyn Bailey for nearly
four months in a rubber raft after their yacht had been
sunk by a sperm whale is quite extraordinary, especially
as they started with little drinking water and no
conventional equipment for catching fish. They lived
all this time almost as sea creatures themselves, forced to
use their brains to make up for their lack of natural
physical abilities. Maralyn could not even swim.

They were living in a particularly interesting part of
the ocean, as their yacht sank some 250 miles from the
Galápagos Islands. They drifted about 1500 miles in a
mainly north-westwards direction for 118 days across an
area of the Pacific Ocean known as the tropical
convergence, where an upwelling current produced frequent
rain and an astonishing variety of marine life.

The Baileys both felt strongly that these creatures
had as much right to live as human beings (indeed after
the collision Maralyn's first thoughts were for the injured

10

suggested that we should alter course to miss the ship. There was in fact little danger on our present course but I agreed and sheered off a little. When the ship was abeam its searchlight played for a few moments on our sails and we pondered as to what type of fisherman it was. Only many hours later did we connect our own misfortune with the idea that it must have been a whaler. With the ship well astern of us I turned into my bunk glad to have relief from the irksome business of trying to stay awake at night.

After what seemed only minutes I became aware of Maralyn shaking me.

"It's your watch," she said. "Seven o'clock."

The sun was just rising above the horizon and Maralyn had already started the stove to begin our usual pleasant breakfast routine. I had barely roused myself when we felt a jolt on the port side which shook the boat with a report like a small explosion. Alarmed, Maralyn dashed on deck whilst I, now fully awake, followed up behind having clambered over the bunk lee-board.

"It's a whale," Maralyn cried, "and it's injured!" I reached the deck to see the monster threshing wildly off our stern leaving a red trail of blood in the water. It was our most

terrifying moment: that great tail, at any second, could smash
our boat. Maralyn said, "Have we damaged it?", not realizing
that it was probably we who were the more seriously hurt.
The whale with its tail whipping the surface of the sea into
foam suddenly sounded leaving us alone on a blood reddened
ocean in awesome silence.

"Never mind the whale," I exclaimed. "What damage has
it done to us?"

Water was already above the cabin sole which hindered my
search for the damage, but I soon found a hole about
eighteen inches long by some twelve inches wide below the
water line just abaft the galley on the port side. Almost
speechless with shock I examined the hole and tried to think
clearly what to do. Maralyn was already at the bilge pump.

"Get that spare jib sheet with the heavy snap shackle," I
shouted.

Maralyn, alive to the danger now, obeyed with promptness.
I struggled forward to retrieve a headsail and Maralyn
followed.

We trimmed the sails to heel the boat and keep her moving
forward at about two to three knots. On the foredeck Maralyn
clipped the sheet to the corner of the headsail while I bunched

14

up the luff and lowered the sail over the bow making sure that enough of the sheet had been paid out to clear the keel. We dragged the sail aft to cover the hole and I clipped the luff on to the port life-line whilst Maralyn made the sheet fast to starboard.

We scrambled aft and pumped furiously for ten minutes in an effort to keep down the water level.

"The water isn't going down," gasped Maralyn. "Let's try blankets—push them into the hole!"

Even then we could not believe that the yacht would sink. We rammed the blankets into the hole, but it was no good. The water was still rising. Perhaps there was more damage elsewhere? Perhaps it was the shape of the hull with its twin keels which was causing our makeshift collision-mat fail to stem the flow.

Barely forty minutes had passed since we had felt the first shock and we now stared at each other in disbelief.

"We'll have to abandon her."

With the realization that saving *Auralyn* was now beyond our powers we suddenly knew just how much we had come to love that boat. We felt no fear. We had no doubts at all about our chances in the life-raft. We were close to a shipping route; there would be no problem. I set about releasing the Avon life-raft and the small inflatable rubber dinghy whilst Maralyn began to collect together a few essentials of food and gear. She threw as much as she could grab into two sail bags and together with our emergency kit transferred them to the life-raft. I began to collect all the water containers I could find and tossed them into the dinghy. We worked fast and in silence. There was no panic.

The fifty minutes since the whale attack seemed to us then a lifetime. We left *Auralyn* for the last time. We felt sick at heart and stupefied watching everything we had worked for sink slowly until the tip of the mast disappeared beneath the waves with fearful finality.

There was no other life we had wanted than to be free to sail our own boat across the oceans of the world. Now it had all gone—our dreams, our great adventure. It was as though life had stopped. Nothing seemed important any more.

But the greatest adventure was yet to come.

The strain shows in Maurice's face as he glances back at me and *Auralyn* settles low in the water.

While Maurice rowed the dinghy, I took pictures of the sinking of our beloved *Auralyn*.

18

20

Auralyn settled and slowly disappeared beneath the Pacific Ocean.

2 Adrift and Alone

Maurice

March 4th   *Auralyn* had finally disappeared and we felt very much alone in that wide ocean. There was nothing left to show her going but the loose equipment that had floated free. Neither of us spoke; each left the other alone with their thoughts. Maralyn kept herself busy by putting the raft in some sort of order, whilst I rowed the dinghy amongst the debris and retrieved four containers of water, one of kerosene and one of methylated spirits (alcohol). Rowing over to the raft I made the dinghy fast with two twenty-five foot lines and then paid out the sea-anchor and made that fast to the raft. My movements were slow and laborious, mentally I was in a state of shock and low spirits.

I rested and looked across at Maralyn. She was weeping. For the first time in my life I felt utter despair, utter helplessness.

"I rowed the dinghy amongst the debris . . ."

22

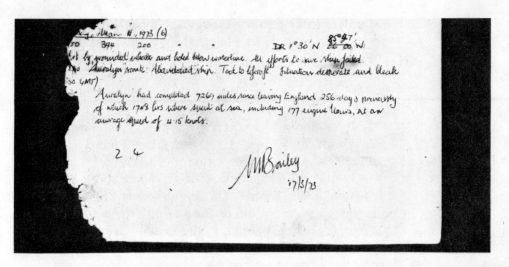

Maurice Bailey's cryptic entry in the log book says "Hit by wounded whale and holed below waterline. All efforts to save ship failed. *Auralyn* sank. Abandoned ship. Took to life-raft. Situation desperate and bleak."

"We're near a shipping lane," I said with a confidence I did not feel. "We'll be seen soon."

Maralyn stopped her work and looked up and said softly, "I was planning to have a plaque engraved in New Zealand, saying thank you to *Auralyn* for carrying us so safely, and to fix it to the main hatch." She paused and then said, "It has all gone . . . everything we have worked for . . . now we have nothing."

It was heartbreaking. *Auralyn* had been more than just a boat to us, she had been a friend and companion—our home.

There was no recrimination, Maralyn was wonderful. She did not blame me for our desperate plight. Yet I blamed myself and I probed my mind to find exactly what I had done wrong. Was there something more that I could have done to have saved the ship? Everything appeared confused just before we abandoned *Auralyn* and now with the clarity generated from hindsight I imagined that, with a little more effort, I could have saved her. I think that I was mistaken, nothing could have saved that boat.

23

Maralyn broke into my thoughts, "What do you think of our chances?" she asked. I felt that I must give her hope.

"Fairly good," I said. "How much food and water have we got?"

"Enough for twenty days, with careful rationing," she replied.

"Give us another ten days without food and water, we could last for thirty days," I said with false jubilance. "Surely, someone is bound to see us within four weeks."

"Do you think we shall be missed?" Maralyn asked.

"It is possible," I said. "Though no one in England would be expecting to hear from us for a month or two."

We sat for several minutes in silence sadly reflecting on our friends in England when my thoughts turned gradually to those others whom we had met already on our voyage and who were now still sailing across the Pacific.

"Odwin and Ellie in *Vahine* will surely realize that something is wrong when we don't turn up in Wreck Bay," I said eventually. *Vahine* was a German yacht that had sailed from Panama for the Galápagos the day before we did.

"Then of course Mike in *Carmen* would know we had sailed from Panama and when he arrives in Wreck Bay he will wonder where we are," Maralyn spoke enthusiastically. Mike was an Australian single-hander. Maralyn went on, "They will surely report that we are overdue to the authorities and then they will start to search for us."

This was probably the most bitter blow of all to our morale because even if it did occur to our friends that our absence was strange, they would be just as likely to think that we had arrived at one of the other islands. Our paths might easily not cross again in the Galápagos Islands and I told Maralyn so. "Even if they did start to search for us just try and imagine the impossibility of the task," I said. "They would not even know where to start." We fell silent again. The mental numbness that we felt made conversation difficult at that time.

"I am glad that this happened to us and not to Neville and Sheila," Maralyn said after some time. These were friends who were also sailing to New Zealand, but with their young

24

March 4th   family, in their yacht *Golden Kowhai*.

I could not look at her and betray the despair that must have shown in my face. I wondered what death, when it came, would be like. I hoped that it would be quick and painless—for both of us together.

Maralyn was unable to relieve my dejection. I had already convinced myself that there was little hope of our rescue. What was the sense of creating false hopes? Why was it not possible to have made the correct decision? If only I had left Panama twenty-four hours later, as we had originally planned. If only I had taken a more southerly course, as I should have done. If only . . .

"What would you like for breakfast?" Maralyn asked.

Bringing the two inflatable craft together, I tumbled into the life-raft. Breakfast consisted of a few biscuits liberally smeared with margarine and we sat eating together in silence, thinking. We would certainly get very hungry on these rations.

"What on earth can we do to keep ourselves occupied?" I asked after a time. Maralyn said she had salvaged two books—'Richard III' by Murray and 'Voyaging' by Eric Hiscock and two dictionaries. I groaned, what a selection. However much I was interested in history, I felt that this was not the time and place for a tome like 'Richard III' and I had already read Hiscock from cover to cover.

"We can use these books as the basis of a new library when we get home," Maralyn went on.

I felt exasperated. "There is hardly enough room for essential equipment, let alone books." I must have sounded like a peevish child.

"Never mind," she said. "We can read them and analyse them line by line and discuss them."

She was right of course. They would certainly occupy our minds, but for how long? I examined the contents of the raft. Maralyn had rescued my Nautical Almanac and Sight Reduction Tables for our present latitude. These together with my chart, sextant and deck watch would also help pass the time in efforts to fix our position. She had collected tins of food in two sail bags, two plastic bowls and a bucket, a kit bag

March 4th   full of clothes, the compass, our oilskins, the emergency pack, a torch, my logbook and her diary.

The deck-watch.

These were the cans and utensils that we used for eating and fishing.

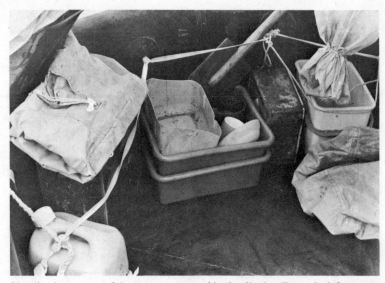

Showing how some of the gear was stowed in the dinghy. From the left a water container, the sextant case with an oilskin jacket on top which Maurice used as pillow, containers for food, the paddle, the gas stove, the bucket for the water catchment, and on the right a sail bag for clothes.

Analysis of the accident

After a time we sat and discussed the accident. How did it happen? We thought about the whale which we identified as a sperm whale of about forty feet or more in length. Although we had not seen the wound, we were certain that it had not been caused by the whale's contact with our hull. The damage to the boat had been caused most probably by its tail. Maralyn, who had the watch, was on deck just before she came below to call me and she had seen nothing of the whale. We were sure that the animal had surfaced almost alongside the boat and had immediately attacked us with its tail. The evidence to support this was the fact that we saw no blood other than in the vicinity of the boat.

What, then, had caused the injury and why should it have attacked us? Our thoughts now turned towards the fishing boat we had passed only four hours previously. We had noted its size, its activity, its use of a searchlight and its attendant

March 4th   launch. Our joint opinion was that it must have been a whaling ship and it did not take us long to associate the whaler with our misfortune. We theorized that the whaler, or its launch, had harpooned the whale just before we had sailed past and by some mischance the whale had escaped, injured and angry. It is possible that it had followed us through the rest of the night and revenged itself on our hull at first light. Or, it may have come across us by some very unlucky chance.

Although several alternative theories have been suggested to us, none have to date affected our opinion. It is possible that the accident could have been caused by the whale's affinity to the bright red colour of the antifouling. Again, there was the theory that perhaps the whale had associated our boat with another whale. No alternative theory explains the whale's injury. The impact we felt and the resulting damage did not, we are certain, considering the bulk and fat of the creature, inflict any deep wound.

Also, we cannot rid ourselves of the picture of the whaler and its searchlight. It is quite likely that they were searching for a whale that had just escaped. We noticed that just before the ship dipped below the horizon, three miles away, the whaler put out the searchlight and the majority of its deck lights.

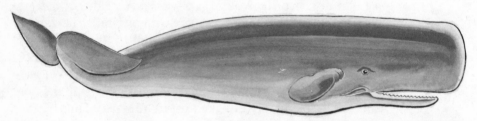

Sperm Whale. The type of whale which collided with *Auralyn*. They grow to sixty-five feet long, feed on fish, particularly squid. We usually saw them in pairs. The fatty tissue lying above the bones of the upper jaw is known as the spermaceti organ which produces a kind of wax used in the preparation of some medical and cosmetic products. Ambergris, a solid waxy substance found in the whale's rectum, is extremely valuable and used as a base to hold volatile scents.

28

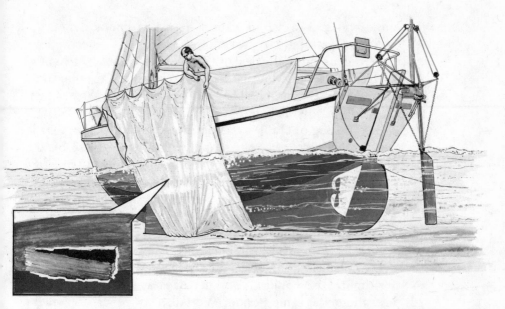

This drawing shows the position of the hole made by the whale and also the way we tried to plug the hole from the outside using a sail as a collision mat. The bilge keel interfered with its efficiency and there might also have been other damage which we were unable to locate.

Maralyn

Sorting out our gear

Our world was now so small. I arranged the few possessions we had salvaged round the outside of the raft so as to leave room in the centre for us to sit. After the initial burst of tears, I was only able to think of the matter in hand and found it easier if I concentrated fully on the present task.

We stayed around the immediate area for quite a time and picked up a few items which had floated up from the depths, but surprisingly, very little wreckage appeared. Maurice rowed the dinghy back and forth and picked up two pencils, a tin of margarine, a jar of Coffee-mate, a small container of methylated spirits, one gallon of kerosene and four water carriers each containing one gallon. We were pleased to pick up the water as it increased our meagre supply. Maurice had

29

March 4th   only managed to get six gallons into the dinghy before the boat had sunk but now we had ten.

Within an hour all trace of the boat had vanished from the surface of the sea. Maurice arranged the gear in the dinghy as I sorted out the raft. I lashed the sextant in one corner then wedged the polythene bowls containing our tinned food next to it. The bag of clothes was on the other side with a plastic bowl containing our books and diaries and finally by the entrance two one-gallon water containers.

There was nothing else to do and I persuaded Maurice to come into the raft where we had shelter from the sun's direct rays, but not from the heat.

As we sat through that first afternoon we talked quietly for several hours assessing our position. Using a blank page of my diary I made a list of all the food we had. By careful rationing I estimated we could last twenty days and the water would last about the same period. We talked of other shipwrecks and Maurice remembered an incident where the people had been picked up after twenty days and the longest time he could remember people drifting for was approximately ninety days.

I was quite optimistic. I had followed Maurice's plots all the way from Panama and knew we were not that far from the Galápagos Islands. When you have sailed thousands of miles across oceans a mere three hundred miles seems nothing, only three or four days sailing at the most! Maurice was not so optimistic as he had better knowledge of currents and winds and realized the gravity of our position although he didn't let on to me.

Salvaged equipment   (* = items left when rescued)

2 Blue bowls*	2 Sail bags*
1 Round bucket	2 Oilskin jackets and trousers*
1 Oblong bucket*	1 Binoculars
1 Plastic wastepaper basket	1 Tilley lamp
2 Cushions	1 Mallet
2 Towels	1 Sextant*
1 Camera*	1 Compass

30

March 4th

2 Books	1 Deck-watch*
2 Dictionaries*	Navigation books*
1 Camping Gaz stove*	Ship's papers and Log*
1 Torch	2 Diaries*
1 Scissors*	Mariner's knife and
1 Pliers*	marline spike
2 Plates (1*)	1 Box safety matches
2 Mugs (1*)	2 Pencils
2 Saucepans (small) (1*)	1 Felt pen (found in
1 Bag clothes*	Maralyn's oilskin pocket)

Emergency bag including: First-aid kit, knife, fork and spoon each, penknife, small walking compass, vitamin tablets, glucose, Heinz baby food, nuts, dates, peanuts, water bottles (and should have contained fishing equipment).

Salvaged food

2 tins	Steak and kidney pie filling	2 tins	Carnation evaporated milk
1 tin	Ambrosia rice pudding	2 tins	Carnation condensed milk
2 tins	Fray Bentos steak and kidney pudding	1 tin	Tate & Lyle treacle
2 tins	Tyne Brand minced beef	1 tin	Big-D peanuts
2 tins	Wall's braised steak	4 tins	Heinz baby foods
		1 pkt	Whitworth's brazil nuts
1 tin	Sainsbury's ravioli	$\frac{1}{2}$ pkt	Dates
1 tin	Curry	1 bottle	Boots multivite vitamin tablets
3 tins	Sardines		
1 tin	Wall's pork luncheon meat	$\frac{1}{2}$ jar	Carnation Coffee-mate
1 tin	Ham and egg roll	$\frac{1}{2}$ jar	Robertson's marmalade
6 tins	Campbell's spaghetti bolognaise	4 pkts	Carr's biscuits
		$\frac{1}{2}$ sm. jar	Boots glucose powder
1 tin	Blue Band margarine	1	Huntley & Palmers Dundee cake

3 *Auralyn*, Maralyn and Me

Maurice

The beginning of our adventure

It had all started, I suppose, when I first met Maralyn. She supplanted my love of mountains, gliding and sailing. In fact the money I had saved from my salary as a printer's clerk to join a syndicate to buy a sailplane now went towards buying a house. During our early married life there was very little money to spare for these other pastimes. Even Maralyn's earnings as a tax officer did not provide much spare cash for the activities we liked most. Nevertheless, we considered ourselves fortunate in having our own house and we found much pleasure in those first years in the domesticated business of developing our home and garden.

I yearned still for a means of escaping from the tediousness of suburban life. As though some latent adventurous spirit was awakening in her, Maralyn began to enthuse over the sea and the mountains. I could do little to interest her in flying; the vision of leaving the ground in a frail machine was a frightening prospect for her.

We discussed outdoor activities and we began making frequent trips to the Peak district, the Lake district and Scotland, climbing and walking and camping a great deal. There was no greater joy than the mutual fascination we found in the solitude of those sombre mountains.

As for the sea, it was a different matter. We just could not afford a boat. Prices of yachts were rising faster than my salary increases and, as only a small proportion of my income could be devoted to our 'boat fund', we could see little prospect of buying a boat in the near future.

But Maralyn discovered a way one cold and wet November

evening in 1966. "Suppose," she said turning away from her
silent contemplation of the rain streaming down the window,
"that we sold our house, bought a yacht and lived on board."
The idea sounded impossible and I said so, thus disguising my
reluctance to give up the tenuous security we had already
achieved. "You're not even trying," she retorted and began to
outline her ideas, not only for buying a boat, but for an
ambitious voyage to New Zealand. In short, her arguments
finally won me over.

The boat we wanted needed to have a minimum length of
thirty feet, a moderate draught, full headroom, ample beam,
high freeboard and the ability to steer herself easily. It very
soon became clear that we could not get all these without
having a boat built to our specific requirements. Even then
compromise, an essential feature of life, meant some modification of our ideals.

The yacht that most nearly met our specification was an
auxiliary sloop called a 'Golden Hind', designed by Maurice
Griffiths and built in Plymouth by Hartwell's. It had a
plywood hull with double chines, a shallow draught, twin
keels and was thirty-one feet overall.

Having discussed the project at length we then ordered
our boat from the builders for delivery during the spring of
1968. Now that we were committed, Maralyn showed her
usual thoroughness by working out a timetable for the yacht's

At Southampton before we left on our voyage.

33

fitting out and victualling. At the same time I arranged for the sale of our house in Derby and looked for a job in towns on the south coast. I eventually found a position with the Camelot Press, a Southampton firm of book printers.

We called our boat *Auralyn*, a combination of our two names. Her delivery coincided with my change of jobs and we immediately started work preparing for the voyage at Moody's boatyard at Swanwick. We lived on board during all

Auralyn on the hard at Moody's yard when fitting out.

Auralyn leaving the Hamble River at the start of her fateful voyage.

The voyage begins this time, sharing our living space with the timber and tools necessary for all the alterations we carried out. Every spare moment was taken with the work of reconstruction and modification of our boat.

The start of our voyage was planned for 1970 but twice we had to put off our departure; first due to the death of Maralyn's father after a long illness, and then because Maralyn had to get treatment for arthritis in her shoulders.

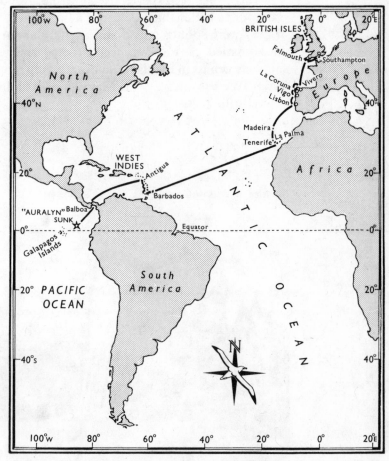

This shows *Auralyn*'s outward track from the Hamble River, near Southampton, to her sinking position near the Galápagos Islands in the Pacific.

To the Caribbean   Our voyage of adventure started in late June 1972, from the Hamble River and we sailed to ports in Spain and Portugal, then to Madeira, the Canary Islands and across the Atlantic Ocean to the West Indies. These were happy times for us and we made many friends among the adventurous souls from many countries sailing the same route. The tensions and stresses of shore life slipped away leaving us with the contentment and tranquillity which the manning of a sailing ship at sea always brings.

Auralyn behaved perfectly and she responded to our promptings better than we could have wished. Small failures of gear were soon rectified and nothing about her performance worried us. Life was well ordered and we worked the ship between us in regular watches, sharing the more onerous duties. We became very fit, Maralyn also finding relief from her arthritic pains.

Maurice on deck whilst cruising in the Caribbean.

36

Maralyn takes a sun sight. The life-raft, which was to be such an important item of *Auralyn*'s gear, is stowed on the cabin top behind her.

Early February 1973 found us in Panama preparing for our Pacific Ocean crossing. We worked hard overhauling the rigging and repainting the boat. We laid aboard provisions to last nine months and extra fuel to enable us to motor through the doldrums if necessary.

Overriding this activity were our thoughts on the prospect of our Pacific crossing. The enormity of our undertaking now struck us forcibly and we were thorough with our preparations. Once more ready for sea *Auralyn* tugged at her moorings, looking splendid, freshly painted, provisioned and complete in every detail.

And so we set off again—but this time towards disaster.

4 Settling In

Maralyn

March 4th   We settled into the raft as comfortably as possible and before the sun rose too high we had our breakfast which consisted of four biscuits each spread thickly with margarine and a smear of marmalade. At lunch time we had a small handful of peanuts each and our evening meal was one tin of food between us.

At the last moment as I left the yacht I had grabbed our small 'Camping Gaz' butane stove. Unfortunately, the gas

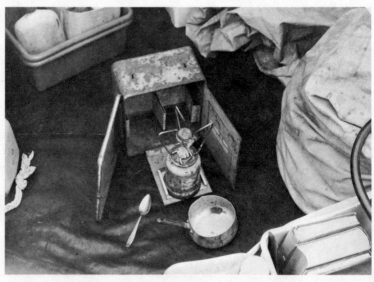

The gas stove which we carried in the raft for the whole period even though the cartridge was exhausted after a few days.

We had two of these bottles, one of them would contain our day's ration in the early period of the voyage.

canister was part used and we had no spare cartridges, but by careful use I reckoned it would last out our supply of tins. I put the contents of a tin in a small saucepan we had managed to salvage and heated the food for three or four minutes. I took one spoonful then handed the pan to Maurice who also took one spoonful. We shared it like this until the food had gone. At meal times all conversation ceased and we concentrated on our food. When the last mouthful had disappeared we were both still very hungry and occasionally for 'afters' we would raid the biscuit tin and have one each, or sometimes a date, and drool over its sweetness.

In our emergency kit I had placed two plastic bottles each holding two pints of water and one of these bottles would be our day's ration. When it was empty we would fill it from the main supply kept in the dinghy. For breakfast we would stir approximately three spoons of Coffee-mate into a cup of water and the rest of the day we would take turns and have sips from the bottle, finishing the rest after our evening meal. We learned later that our thirst might have been better satisfied if we had drunk our ration at one go.

On leaving the yacht I had rescued two books, one was Eric Hiscock's 'Voyaging' which he had kindly autographed for me one day on the Hamble River. The second book was a historical volume, 'Richard III' by Paul Kendall Murray. We passed many hours remembering the books we had left behind and usually by starting with the words, "Did you read . . .", we would tell each other the story in minute detail. I remembered one story of the life of Eleanor of Aquitaine; she was imprisoned for sixteen years by her husband and the way in which she kept her mind occupied during that time was fascinating. Another story was of an American soldier captured during the Korean war who was kept in solitary confinement yet retained his sanity by designing and building in his mind his future home. It was this last story that gave us the idea of designing and planning our next boat in every detail.

Maurice

The sun rose higher and the heat became intense and with it a state of languor pervaded the raft. I opened the chart and plotted our Dead Reckoning position. We were, in fact, quite close to the shipping lane. I estimated our position to be 1° 30′ N 85° 47′ W, 250 miles north of Ecuador and 300 miles east of the Galápagos Islands, which was too far north to allow the west going current to drift us on to the islands.

The wind blew from the south-east and, although light in strength, would drive us even farther north. Could we, perhaps, row the hundred or so miles south to the latitude of the Galápagos? It would take us about twelve days to reach the longitude of the Galápagos drifting at twenty-five miles per day. We would then have to row ten miles per day south to offset the wind and current and to reach their latitude at the same time as attaining the longitude. These calculations depended a lot on the wind and current remaining constant. Were we capable of rowing the dinghy ten miles each day with the raft in tow? Should we abandon the raft to give ourselves a better chance?

I stopped thinking about this problem and contented myself with the knowledge that in the next few days we should be

40

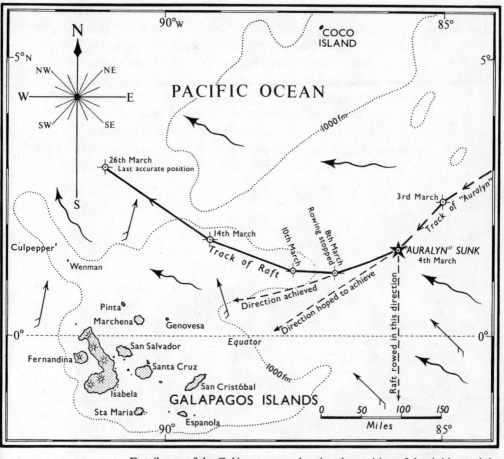

Detail map of the Galápagos area showing the position of the sinking and the track of the raft in the few days afterwards. Feathered arrows are prevailing winds. Curly arrows are currents.

drifting in a shipping lane. Nevertheless, I would have to mention the possibility of rowing to Maralyn. But later; not now.

We noticed a slight loss of pressure in the raft during the afternoon and I pumped air into the tubes with the pump provided in the raft's emergency kit. This made me aware of the appalling vulnerability of our position; only our two small craft to keep us afloat on that vast ocean.

The raft consisted principally of two superimposed circular inflated tubes giving four and a half feet internal diameter. A floor was attached around the lower perimeter of the bottom tube. Below the raft was fixed a CO_2 bottle and three stabilizing pockets. A semi-circular inflated tube that bridged the raft was fixed to the top tube and this supported a bright, orange coloured canopy covering the whole raft.

There was a flap to cover the entrance and opposite this was a ventilation and look-out aperture protected by a skirt. Two non-return topping-up valves were situated just inside the

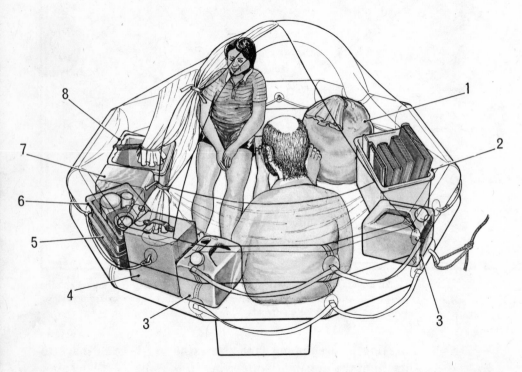

This detail drawing shows how the gear was arranged within the raft, and how we sat when we were resting. The items are as follows: 1. Sail bag containing clothes; 2. Plastic bowl containing navigation books, etc.; 3. Plastic one-gallon water containers; 4. Box containing sextant; 5. Box bowl containing cans of food with, fitted on top of it; 6. Plastic bowl containing eating utensils, fishing gear, and water bottles; 7. 'Camping Gaz' butane gas stove in container; 8. Plastic bucket used for catching water. See also the photograph on page 27 for the actual gear as it was stowed in the raft.

This photograph taken in the English Channel shows how the raft and dinghy looked when they were afloat during the voyage. The oar carries a pair of oilskin trousers acting as a flag and proved to be considerably more visible than the rest of the raft or dinghy.

entrance, one for the lower tube, the other for the upper and 'bridge' tubes. Life-lines were fixed around the raft on the outside. The raft was made of black natural rubber proofed material. Apart from the pump the raft was equipped with two paddles, a repair kit, a length of orange polythene line and a quoit.

The dinghy, made of heavier grey, rubberized fabric, was boat-shaped, about nine feet overall and was divided into two separate flotation chambers with an inflated seat or thwart attached amid-ships. It had two fixed rubber rowlocks, two oars and a bellows type pump.

43

March 4th   During the late afternoon I explained to Maralyn the desperate half-formed plan to row south to reach the latitude of the Galápagos Islands.

"We'll have to do the rowing at night," she said, "it would be impossible in the heat of the day."

I was depressed by the seriousness of our position and reluctant to make any decision. I found myself renouncing all pretence of leadership, and with her flair for organization Maralyn was taking command. "If it is too dark to see the compass we can steer by the stars," she said simply. Maralyn appeared undaunted. "We'll start rowing immediately after supper. Two-hour spells will be enough." I hated the idea of rowing and asked, "How far do you think you can row in two hours?" She would not be discouraged. "We must try," she said.

The day wore on and the sun slid towards the clear horizon bringing the refreshing coolness we longed for. After our evening meal I argued a case for deferring rowing until the next evening. It was not just laziness that made me argue like this. We were drifting towards the shipping lane which runs to the south of the Galápagos. In another twenty-four hours we should be in the centre of this lane and we might just see a ship.

Of course this was wrong, we should have started rowing straight away. The longer we delayed, the more we would have to row on subsequent nights. We settled down for our first night adrift, making ourselves as comfortable as possible. Unable to lie down in the raft together, one of us would curl up on the floor and sleep, whilst the other keeping watch, would sit hunched up in the little remaining space. We would change over every three hours. Maralyn had the worst of the arrangement because, whether sleeping or watch-keeping, I would take up the most room. We found this arrangement satisfactory only when the raft was inflated hard. The watch-keeper therefore had to pump the raft frequently to replace any slight loss of pressure. When several weeks later the raft became damaged and it was impossible to keep fully inflated, we abandoned this system and slept fitfully where we sat.

44

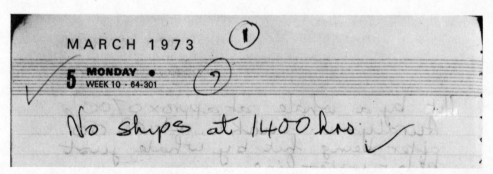
NB.   See publisher's note on page 9.

Dawn arrived and heralded another scorching day. We used some of our precious food, but hardly enough to sustain us, and sipped our daily one pint ration of water carefully. Even then we found our thirst intolerable but hunger, up to then, was bearable. I examined the water containers in the dinghy and was horrified to discover that four gallons had been contaminated by sea water. It was obvious that we had to have rain soon to replace this foul water.

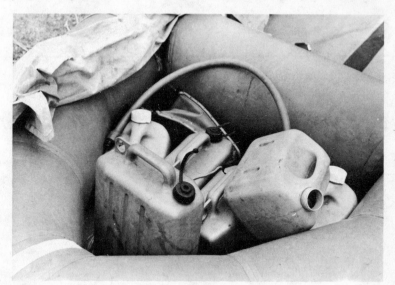

The water containers and the bellows were stowed in the forward part of the dinghy.

45

March 5th   That night after retrieving the drogue we started rowing.
(1)   The task of towing the unwieldy bulk of the raft was slow, painful and laborious; we strained our bodies and badly blistered our hands. At each stroke the dinghy would be propelled forward at a good pace, only to be brought up short when the painter between the two craft tautened, thus

When the moon was up we used the compass to check our course.

46

Rowing the
dinghy

braking any further progress. The raft, responding to the momentum, would then slowly, Oh! so slowly and sluggishly, move forward for a short distance. Hour followed laborious hour.

When the moon was up we checked our course with the compass, afterwards we used the stars, using principally the constellations of Orion, Crux and the Plough, with the Pole Star low on the northern horizon.

Eight hours rowing had exhausted us and we found that even though we doubled our water ration we did not find any relief from our thirst. This was indeed a bad thing. I doubted our ability to row enough each night to attain the right latitude before our water ran out. Although she had suffered through this strenuous activity, Maralyn did not complain and I could not disillusion her.

6 TUESDAY WEEK 10 · 65-300 Shrove Tuesday. ⑧

No ships at 13.30. Heard 1 plane last night — no sign of it — Rowed turn & turn about thro' the cool hours & the night — exhausted

During the day I took sextant altitude sights of the sun from the dinghy; a morning sight for a position line and a noon sight for our latitude. The continual movement of the dinghy, the ocean swell, and the horizon being under two miles distant because my eye was only three feet above the sea, made accurate observations impossible. The declination of the sun was daily getting farther north and within a few more days it would be in the proximity of our latitude and would be useless for finding our position because the sextant angle would be too wide. The northern summer was fast approaching and with it, Maralyn reminded me, the wet season.

My calculations showed that we had only gained a little over four miles to the south, whilst our westerly drift had been nearly thirty miles. I could say nothing to Maralyn; she was very optimistic. In fact, later in the day, when a layer of cumulus cloud appeared on the horizon to the south-west, she was convinced that it lay over the Galápagos Islands.

I kept a check on the accuracy of my wrist-watch by frequent comparisons with the compass and ensuring that the sun's maximum altitude coincided with the hands showing twelve o'clock. The accuracy of the watch helped me a lot when waiting to take a noon latitude sextant sight.

This watch, a Rotary Incabloc, was hung on the electric cable of the emergency light, which itself was out of action because the battery was broken, and Maralyn would sometimes catch her hair on the winder which pulled it out and stopped the watch. This was frustrating as our day was organized around the time taken from this watch. Although it was nearly nine years old and repeatedly saturated with water, it kept remarkably good time. To start the watch again I would wait until the sun attained its maximum altitude, which I found with the sextant, and then set the hands of the watch to twelve o'clock and start it again. Although we placed little

Maurice's wrist watch hung from the bridge tube of the life-raft.

reliance on its absolute accuracy, we were indeed surprised to discover that it was only two minutes slow when we were rescued.

During the day we would get an idea of our drift or the wind direction by using the watch as a compass. This was especially helpful after we later lost the boat's compass when the dinghy capsized.

Our efforts at rowing were continued on the third and fourth nights and then, having fixed our position at noon on the fifth day, I explained to Maralyn my misgivings about rowing any more. Surprisingly she agreed, saying that the sooner we drifted into a shipping lane the better.

"You will not find these lanes full of shipping like the English Channel," I said. "Months may pass before a ship will be seen."

"But there will be a chance," Maralyn replied emphatically.

Maralyn

For three nights we had rowed in turn, two hours each throughout the coolness of the evening until the sun rose the next morning. We had taken the ship's compass from the cockpit and Maurice had wedged it between the water carriers and we followed a compass course when there was enough light from the moon. After that we steered by the stars.

At the end of this time we were both exhausted and had blisters on our hands. A feature of this exercise was our alarming consumption of water. I had laid down the ration as one pint of water each per day, as I knew that one of the most dangerous things to do was to let the body dehydrate and this was about the least amount our bodies would need. However, we found that during these three days we were exceeding our ration. It was then that Maurice explained the true position to me. We had only managed by rowing to gain ten miles south and we would have to row for, at least, another ten to twelve days to attain sufficient southing to keep on the same latitude as the Galápagos Islands—but the current was taking us west faster than we rowed south. This, in simple terms, meant that however hard we rowed we would still pass north of the Galápagos Islands.

Maurice

March 9th
(5)

Maralyn brooded for some time and left the raft and clambered into the dinghy. Picking up the oars she thrust them upright down each side of the thwart and guyed them fore and aft with a thin line. Between these two 'masts' she rigged a sail bag as a sail.

In the light south-east wind the sail worked well. "You'll be driving us north-west," I said.

"And towards a shipping lane—and towards the American coast!" Maralyn retorted.

What could I say? It was no use explaining that once we were out of the doldrum belt we would meet the north-east trade winds again and these would drive us south-west away from the American continent. There was only one thing that I could really hope for and that was to meet a possible counter current running east just north of the cold Humboldt current.

Soon after Maralyn had fixed the sail we encountered an electrical storm; more picturesque than violent. The sky was lit by momentary flashes of light charging from the tall and majestic cumulo-nimbus clouds that now towered above us. Thunder rolled over us like loud and tumultuous gunfire. Yet there was no rain. The display soon finished and left us fractionally cooler.

The four days that followed were even hotter; the sun shining from an almost cloudless sky; there was no wind. We wilted during the hottest part of the day under the raft's canopy, trying to keep cool by means of evaporation, draping our bodies with our spare clothes soaked in sea water. Drop by drop we conserved our depleting water supply.

Our main hope of survival now was to meet a ship. We kept

a strict watch, two hours each throughout the day and night and reasoned that, with the colossal amount of shipping going through the Panama Canal, at least one ship would pass our way.

What I had failed to comprehend was the vastness of that ocean and the fact that we were a mere speck of human flotsam.

'A' lost a week ago today.

We are still well but V. tired
as it is impossible to rest or
sleep properly & the mental anguish
doesn't help.
Our bottoms are getting spotty &
sore.
- Rigged a sail on the dinghy oars &
hope it will take us ↖ (NNE)
a little & not further out into the
Pacific - the ocean looks V wide & lonely.
The chronometer clicked & stopped for
a while but is going again.
~~Liferaft floor has several leaks~~ -m mended
one, but inside keeps getting wet.NOTES

We are getting very hungry
& the ~~food~~ we eat
doesn't seem to fill us.
B/Fast - consists of biscuits
spread with a blob of
marguere & water with coffeemate
lunch - Biscuits & water & a few nuts
Every - 1 tin meat

We are drinking about 1pt each pr day the
heat is bad especially from midday - 4 pm

FEBRUARY			
S	4	11	18	25
M	5	12	19	26
T	6	13	20	27
W	7	14	21	28
T	1	8	15	22
F	2	9	16	23
S	3	10	17	24

MARCH				
S	4	11	18	25
M	5	12	19	26
T	6	13	20	27
W	7	14	21	28
T	1	8	15	22	29
F	2	9	16	23	30
S	3	10	17	24	31

APRIL				
S	1	8	15	22	29
M	2	9	16	23	30
T	3	10	17	24
W	4	11	18	25
T	5	12	19	26
F	6	13	20	27
S	7	14	21	28

MAY				
S	6	13	20	27
M	7	14	21	28
T	1	8	15	22	29
W	2	9	16	23	30
T	3	10	17	24	31
F	4	11	18	25
S	5	12	19	26

5 First Steps in Survival

Maralyn

So the first week drew to a close. The days had gone fairly quickly as we had managed to keep ourselves occupied and everything was new and strange.

We had seen many prehistoric looking turtles and it amazed us how unafraid of us they were. They would swim in a leisurely fashion round the raft and then disappear underneath. They rubbed and bumped the bottom and emerged again on the other side. After our initial surprise and delight at their presence we began to worry about damage to the raft from the barnacles and, in the case of young turtles, the spines on their backs. Surely continual rubbing would chafe and puncture the thin floor of the raft? Next time one approached we turned it round and pushed it off in the opposite direction. But they were very persistent and returned time and time again. Eventually, of course, we became angry and frustrated and we gave them a clout on the head with one of the raft paddles. This treatment surprised them and kept them at bay for a while but ten minutes later they would return, so it turned out to be a constant running battle between us and the turtles.

The paddle shows damage caused by repeatedly hitting turtles.

I mentioned to Maurice the possibility of catching one and eating it, but as we still had a stock of tinned food, albeit very small, Maurice decided to spare them until it was absolutely necessary to kill.

Maurice

We could not think why turtles should find our raft so congenial. Was it to shelter from the sun, or just to rub themselves on the fabric, ridding themselves of parasites? In the early afternoon when we heard a gasp that invaded the silent world around us, we prepared ourselves for what was usually a very uncomfortable time. Sure enough there was a bump which lifted the sextant case several inches out of place. Followed by another bump towards the centre of the raft, and another . . . It went on with such frequency that our bodies inevitably received a number of blows. Then there was another gasp as a turtle surfaced to breathe.

Almost simultaneously we both now decided to capture this one for its meat.

Maralyn

We were having breakfast in the raft when I saw a ship! I shouted excitedly to Maurice; rescue was at hand! It was about two miles away and closing. In the thin light of the early morning it appeared like a dream ship; only eight days and our ordeal was over!

Maurice climbed into the dinghy and shortened the lines between the two craft. As he was doing this I collected all our flares together and laid them out ready for use. The ship appeared to be a small fishing boat or maybe a private yacht, and, on her present course, she would pass about one mile away.

As she drew level with us Maurice asked for the first flare —

12 MONDAY WEEK 11 · 71-294 ⑧

The liferaft bottom is being chafed by turtles
they seem to have barnacles growing on their
heads. I must try & rub them off on the
raft. Young turtles have small pick-up
spines on their backs. We caught one
small one & I wanted to put it upside down
in the dinghy — to use for food, but it upset
Maurice but we kept it anyway. . gaz
throw him out

A ship passed within 2 mls — we let off
all our flares — 2 were duds — still he
didn't see us. — it was 8 AM. — we
despaired — our 1st ship since the ith Mich
We couldn't believe it — we were so
hopefull for a little while — if only

13 TUESDAY WEEK 11 · 72-293 our luck would change a
little. Chronometer has
broken. 9.
2 whales blew v. close to us last
night. Many sharks around. Wind
has picked up but driving us more
W. than anything — but a breeze keeps
us cooler.

a smoke flare— and with mounting excitement I handed it to
him. He tore off the tape and struck the top with the igniter—
nothing happened. For long seconds we stared at the useless
object and it was with a cry of exasperation that Maurice
threw it into the sea. "It's a dud. A bloody dud!" I handed
him a second flare and this time we both heaved a sigh of
relief as it ignited. As the glow began to diminish I handed
him a second red flare. There was no answering signal from
the ship and she still maintained her course. A third flare was
used—our hopes were fading rapidly.

"How many flares are left?"

"Three, two white and one red."

"Hand me another one—she must see us!" I could see the boat going further and further away. We hadn't been seen. It was pointless using the other two flares.

While Maurice sat dejectedly in the dinghy I began to wave my oilskin jacket although I knew it was no use. After a few minutes Maurice asked me to stop and save my energy and reluctantly I did so. By now the ship's funnel was only visible in the swells on the horizon and before many more minutes had passed the ocean was ours again.

Maurice

I think for the first time in my life I felt true compassion as I saw the disappointment and sadness in Maralyn's eyes. Our morale at this stage took a further plunge, there was nothing to alleviate our despair. We finished our meal in silence. Our position was becoming daily more critical—our food was running low and, if rain did not come soon, water would have to be restricted to about half a pint each per day.

Maralyn

As we rested during the heat of the day we discussed the ship and the reason why she had not seen us and I came to the conclusion that as it was early (8 a.m.) the crew must have been at breakfast, possibly leaving the vessel on auto-pilot.

Then the subject got round to food and inevitably the turtle we still had in the dinghy. Our gas had run out and I had only just managed to warm the tin the previous night. The remaining tins of food would have to be eaten cold. I suggested using the turtle's meat as bait to catch fish to supplement our diet, but unfortunately we had failed to repack the fish hooks and line into our emergency pack at Panama.

56

That evening over our cold meal we agreed that if we wanted to survive we had to kill the turtle and decided the best time was next morning before the sun got too high.

Maurice

At dawn the following morning Maralyn and I sat in the dinghy and planned the killing. Our instruments were simple —a blunt stainless steel mariner's knife, a mild steel penknife honed to some degree of sharpness on a leather sheath, and a pair of stainless steel scissors.

The reptile lay on the floor of the dinghy in a very docile manner. Both of us felt sick at heart, but we had to kill it if we were to live.

"I'll try knocking it out," I said. If it was unconscious I felt it would not struggle and the slaughter might not be too bad.

I lifted the turtle on to the side tube so that its head protruded over the side. I remember my surprise at discovering that, unlike its shore-based brother, the tortoise, its head did not fully retract into the heart-shaped carapace. The head, ugly yet fascinating, had no teeth. Sadly I wished that it would have been possible to have studied the various tortoise species under better circumstances.

Lifting a paddle over my head I brought it down with a resounding crash on to the turtle's skull. Then again, and again. The turtle ceased its movement, it was unconscious. It had not uttered a sound; to our ears it was mute.

The leather sheath for the knife proved to be most valuable as it was the only thing we could use for sharpening the blades.

57

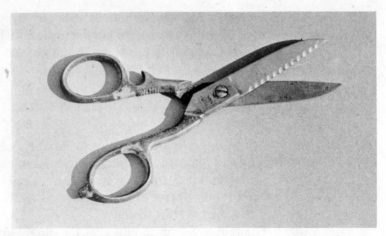

The stainless steel kitchen scissors were used for cutting up fish and turtles.

Maralyn

I knew the only way to kill it was to cut its throat, or decapitate it, and I also knew that I would have to do it as Maurice would have to hold it still. I didn't want to kill it either, it was so friendly and helpless, but we had to be practical and ruthless if we wanted to live. We knew we couldn't put off the deed any longer and I agreed to do the butchery if Maurice could somehow immobilize it.

Maurice stunned the turtle by hitting it over the head with a paddle. It was then held upside down on the dinghy thwart, its head hanging down over a bowl. I then began the gruesome task of slitting its throat. The first stroke of the knife made no impression at all and it took many minutes to hack a small gash in its throat. I expected its skin to be tough but this thick, rubbery, leathery skin was a surprise and our knife totally inadequate for the job.

It was at this point that the turtle came to life again and began to struggle, flailing around with its flippers and claws. I felt an unreasonable anger against the creature for making a difficult job more so and Maurice had a hard task to hold it

58

in place. It took a lot of effort to keep the neck stretched and when the head was half severed I dug deep for the arteries and, as the rich blood spurted over my hands, the turtle ceased its struggle.

The bowl filled with thick red blood and although we had read of people drinking turtle blood, the idea was so revolting that it was emptied into the sea. Immediately, hordes of fish converged on the dinghy and began eating the congealed blood, making loud sucking noises as they greedily devoured the contents of the bowl. I had great difficulty washing my hands as they swarmed towards my fingers as soon as they entered the water.

The next part of the butchery was to remove the lower shell or plastron. After scoring the perimeter deeply, Maurice cut through it with the penknife and eventually we could prise both halves of the shell away leaving the rich white meat exposed. I hacked about four large steaks from each shoulder blade and we slipped the rest of the carcass over the side glad to be rid of the bloody mess and relieved it was all over.

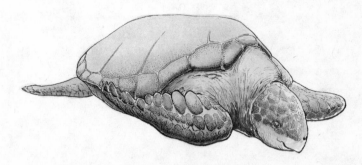

Green Turtle. Takes its name from the green fatty substance found inside. Ridley turtles are very similar and only distinguishable by the markings on the head.

Maurice

Hundreds of fish seized the remaining meat and the blood, and began to devour it all with a terrifying haste.

"We *must* fish," Maralyn said, excited by the sight of so many fish, "And I think I know of a way to do it." She climbed into the raft and after some little time rummaging about, returned to the dinghy clutching the pliers and several stainless steel safety pins. Without another word she cut away the clip portion of one pin and bent it into a small hook. She then threaded thin cord through the spring hoop and tied it with a single-loop Turle knot.

"There," she said triumphantly. Once more Maralyn had displayed her genius at improvisation. I asked, "Where did you find those pins?" She began making another hook, and without looking up answered, "In the first-aid kit. I remembered seeing them when I sorted everything out."

"Do you think they will work?" I asked, immediately regretting the uselessness of the question.

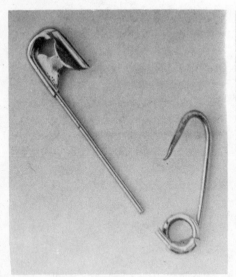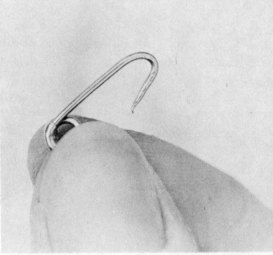

Fish hooks were made by cutting stainless steel safety pins and bending them to shape.

Starting to
fish

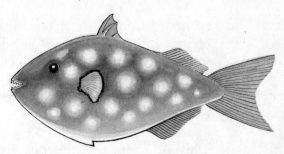

Trigger Fish. So called from the characteristic arrangement of the first two spiny rays of the front dorsal fin. Approximately nine inches long, purple with greyish spots. These fish formed the bulk of our diet.

"We'll soon find out," Maralyn replied and began baiting the hook with a small piece of turtle meat. She dropped the line into the water and the meat was immediately seized by several fish who tore it away from the hook. The meat was so soft that it would not stay on. Maralyn tried again but with no more success. "The meat isn't tough enough," she said in an exasperated voice, "Let's look for some tougher steaks." Our search amongst the meat revealed no coarse flesh, but I noticed that several of the steaks were lined with a membrane.

"Try this," I said, handing Maralyn a piece of meat cut with the membrane attached. Maralyn carefully baited the hook once more, ensuring that the membrane was securely pierced. This time, although the fish pounced upon the meat, it stayed on the hook, and in a very short time Maralyn pulled the line on board with a beautiful silver fish firmly attached to it.

I grabbed the wriggling slippery creature and hit it repeatedly on the back of the head with the mariner's knife until it died. The fish were now in fact taking the hook. Maralyn, without stopping would bait the hook, throw it over the side and land a fish on board. This did not succeed every time, but the fish came in quickly enough to supply us with ample for our morning meal.

The most abundant variety was the flat, somewhat ugly, purple-grey trigger fish, six to nine inches long and oval in shape. Its head occupied nearly half the body, and it had two retractable spines towards the back of the head. The teeth

61

protruded from a relatively small mouth. These fish were to
become our main source of food. They were easy to catch and
simple to cut up and fillet, although we suffered bites from
their teeth and numerous cuts and scratches from their spines.
One or two of these scratches caused septic wounds on my
thumbs.

While Maralyn fished, I would gut the fish and separate the
livers, and hard and soft roes from the females and males
respectively. By the time I had finished, Maralyn had started
cutting away the heads; then I would slit the underside of each
towards the tail. Maralyn followed me by cutting the flesh
away from the backbone so that I could strip the fillets away
from the skin and tail. Finally only one more thing had to be
done. We gouged the eyes out of the head and, sometimes
when fish were scarce and we were hungry, we took the heart
and anything edible out of the head. For our meal we then had
the white-meat steaks, delicacies which we called 'sweetmeats',
or 'poops', as Maralyn would call them, and the eyeballs,
which we found full of thirst satisfying liquid.

To enable us to catch fish for our morning and evening
meals we had to make sure several fish steaks were kept from
each catch for bait. We therefore seized every opportunity to
keep this bait fresh, replacing it whenever we could.

Maralyn

I chopped the fillets into smallish pieces and placed an equal
amount in two bowls. We then returned to the raft and sat
facing each other, our raw meal between us, each waiting for
the other to begin eating. Maurice was the first to take a bite
and tried to encourage me to eat the raw flesh. I ate one fillet
but I couldn't face eating any more. I knew I would have to
conquer the revulsion I felt.

That evening we used the rest of the turtle meat to catch
more fish and this time I managed to eat a little more but not
enough to survive on, but gradually my intake of raw fish
increased until I could almost match Maurice.

62

Maurice

The weather changed soon after our first fishing episode. The wind came boisterously from the south-east, piling the sea into short, steep waves which gave an uncomfortable motion to the raft. All around us the clouds increased. Dare we hope that they would bring rain? None came and our daily wearisome routine of fishing and gutting continued. Our ration of water was barely adequate, and we tried sucking the fish flesh and bones for additional moisture.

It was at this time that Maralyn devised a game of dominoes.

Maralyn

To keep ourselves occupied during the day we read our books, each taking a turn at reading a page out loud. We would then stop and discuss various aspects which would lead often to talking about other things. 'Cat's cradle' amused us for a short time using an odd piece of string. When we tired of this we played word games. Each of us in turn would select a word and using the letters contained in the word we would quietly list all the words of four or more letters we could discover. This kept our minds active and occupied us for several hours, but how I wished I had had the presence of mind to take our pocket chess set. We had no means of making any improvised chess men but we first made dominoes using blank pages out of the log book. The dominoes were cut from strips of paper about 1″ by 2″ and folded into four. We had to play in an unorthodox manner as it was impossible to play correctly by placing each domino end to end; they would have either blown away or been soaked. We each took six pieces representing dominoes and wrote each move on a piece of paper: for instance, I would write down '2 –' (2/blank) and hand Maurice the piece of paper; he would write '– 6' (blank/6) and so we would continue until the game was completed.

March 14th
(10)

During the first two weeks we observed many whales, both sperm and killer whales. Usually they were in pairs and the sperm whales were always closer to us passing about 20 to 30 feet away. I sat anxiously until they had passed.

Our closest contact with a whale whilst adrift was quite remarkable and I can now look back on the occasion and realize it was a unique meeting that very few people have unintentionally experienced. Strangely enough this time the whale was alone, perhaps it was looking for a mate! A huge sperm whale surfaced about 20 feet behind us. I heard the 'whoosh' of air being expelled and put my head through the vent and shouted to Maurice. We stumbled to the entrance to watch the brute's slow advance. It was not going to pass by like all the others. We could find no words to speak, but sat entranced together wondering how the monster would react.

Maurice was very calm and said that there was nothing we could do. He sat by the raft doorway whilst I knelt beside him and I gazed in fascinated horror at this huge creature. It was now so very close; within touching distance. The small round blow-hole looked wet and moist like a dog's nose; it

Killer Whale. Approximately twenty feet long, grey. We usually saw them in twos or threes. They hunt voraciously for their food, often attacking other whales, large fish and seals, hence their name.

64

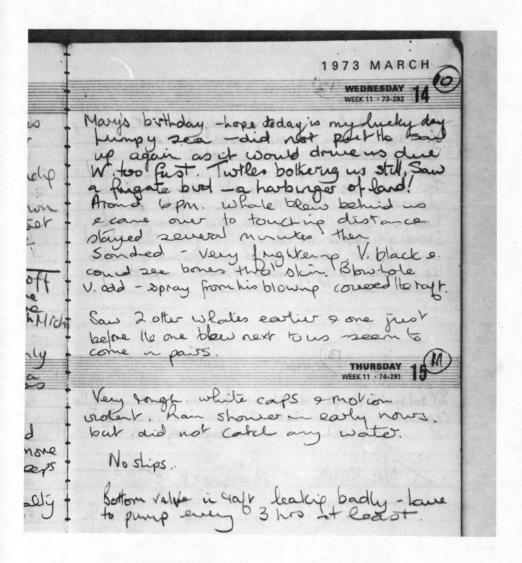

Mary's birthday — hope today is my lucky day
Lumpy sea — did not put the sail
up again as it would drive us due
W. too fast. Turtles bothering us still, Saw
a frigate bird — a harbinger of land!
Around 6 pm. whale blew behind us
& came over to touching distance.
stayed several minutes then
Sounded — very frightening, V. black &
could see bones thro' skin. Blowhole
V. odd — spray from his blowing covered the raft.

Saw 2 other whales earlier & one just
before the one blew next to us seem to
come in pairs.

Very rough. white caps & motion
violent. Rain shower in early hours.
but did not catch any water.

No ships.

Bottom valve in raft leaking badly — have
to pump every 3 hrs at least.

opened slowly and a jet of moisture-laden air, so fine it gave
the appearance of steam, shot into the air and fell like a shower
of rain on the raft.

Maurice tightened his grip on my hand and quietly explained that if the whale tipped the raft over it might be difficult for
him to rescue me. He told me to hold on to the dinghy ropes
and not to let go. I nodded agreement but I don't think his

65

advice really sank in. I think this was the first time that
Maurice was worried about my inability to swim.

We held on to each other as the enormous creature became
stationary alongside. I was biting my lip to stop myself crying
and I remember hearing Maurice saying quietly—"Why
doesn't he go away and leave us in peace." The portion of its
body opposite the doorway was the back and I remember
thinking how cow-like it was—jet black shining with moisture
its ribs showing through the skin. The leviathan maintained
this position for what seemed to us an incredibly long time, in
fact, it was probably no longer than ten minutes but we
expected its fluke to cleave us in two any moment.

At last, as no response was forthcoming to its advances,
the whale started moving away from us and began to sink
below the surface. "Don't dive now," I whispered in the
tenseness of the moment but with a sudden movement its tail
was perpendicular and it disappeared below the surface of the
sea in a near vertical dive with hardly a splash. Our last view
of it was a huge black fan-shaped tail starkly outlined against
a brilliant blue sky. Then it was gone deep into the ocean and
I was left speechless and trembling with the raft rocking
gently as the ripples in the sea subsided.

When whales appeared after this incident I kept a wary eye
on them until we knew they had passed. I would not like to
have a repeat performance!

Maurice

We sat for some minutes looking at the spot where the
whale had vanished. "What a pity we didn't take a photograph. No one will believe us when we talk about it," Maralyn
said eventually. Her confidence in our survival surprised and
also depressed me, and I started hauling the dinghy alongside.
"I think it's time to start fishing for supper," I said. This time
we reversed our roles and I fished.

6 Getting to Know the Turtle

Maurice

March 15th (11)

The day following the whale incident it became much cooler and the wind increased leaving a lumpy, steely-blue sea, and for the first time in the Pacific we saw white caps to the waves. We dropped our sail and for comfort decided to trail the sea-anchor, or drogue, once more. As we began to pay out the warp, we noticed that two of the four canvas loops to which it was fastened had chafed through. There was little we could do to repair them, apart from carefully tying the two chafed parts of each loop together. Even after this attention we realized that the sea-anchor would not last long and, sure enough, the next morning it had disappeared. It was essential to have a sea-anchor and for a substitute I threaded a line through a pair of oilskin trousers and fixed the line in a bight to the lifelines. This slowed our drift down sufficiently to enable us to fish. The raft, with its extra windage, would tend to overtake the dinghy and the warps would become entangled with the CO_2 bottle underneath the raft. This caused the raft to swivel until the entrance faced the oncoming waves, a most vulnerable position for us.

March 16th (12)

Instead of the sail I now attached our second pair of orange oilskin trousers to an oar and wedged this on one side of the dinghy thwart, guying it fore and aft. Should a ship pass, I thought, this 'flag' would help them to spot us.

Maralyn's inventive mind was never at rest and she outlined another idea for amusing ourselves. "Do you think we could make a pack of cards?" she asked, "They would be easier to handle than our dominoes." I agreed and we began cutting up blank leaves from the log book into small rectangles.

Card games   Our playing cards were approximately 2″ by 3″ and it took
at least half a day to make them, drawing the symbols and
numbers in pencil. We had to discipline ourselves not to cheat
since if the cards were held to the light, the pencil markings
showed through very clearly. Unfortunately, because of the
flimsy nature of the cards we were only able to play on fine
days, but it was something to look forward to. We spent many
hours during the next few weeks playing whist.

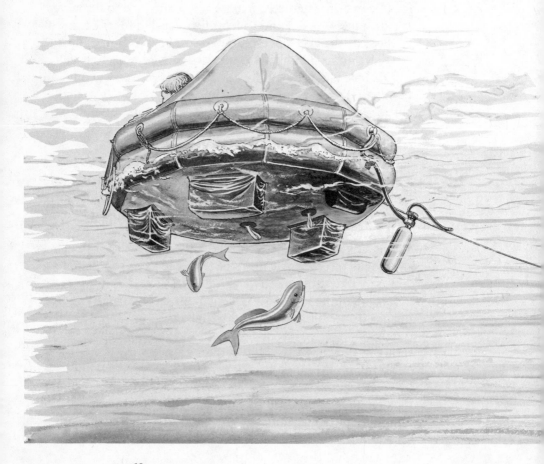

The raft
viewed from
below

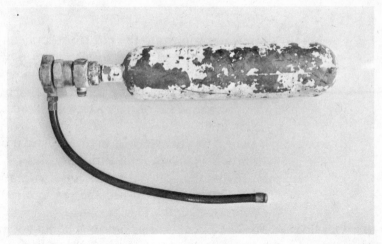

The CO_2 bottle which inflated the raft initially but caused so much trouble thereafter.

A fish's eye view of the underside of the raft together with the sea-anchor, or drogue. The three rectangular objects attached to the underside of the raft are stabilizing pockets. They fill up with water and increase the weight of the raft thus minimizing any tendency for it to capsize in heavy seas. The other hanging object is the CO_2 bottle which escaped from its pocket and hung down under the raft continually getting tangled in the towing line.

69

Maurice

Sea water came into the raft from spray and we were kept busy mopping up the floor with sponges. The lower parts of our bodies had become chafed from contact with the rubber, and left sore patches along our legs and bottoms. We also developed numerous blisters which were caused, we assumed, by salt water.

The next day the weather improved and it became very hot with little wind. Not until three days later did we have any respite from the heat. Then the clouds increased and a strong wind from the south turned the sea into steep, dark foam-flecked moving hills. Then it rained. . . .

Our first rain

We had to collect this precious liquid and noticed that the water ran freely down through the look-out and ventilation aperture, although we had tied the skirt up tightly. Maralyn placed a bucket beneath the opening and the rain water dripped steadily into it. We then had to turn our attention to mopping up the water as it dripped from the inflated tubes where the canopy was attached. This mopping became an exhausting task, especially when we had heavy rainstorms later. About a pint of water had collected in the bucket and we tasted it. It was dreadful; it had been contaminated with the waterproof rubber coating washed from the canopy. We could not drink it and we threw it away. An hour later the water was better and we collected about a pint and transferred it carefully to a plastic container.

One pint of water seemed very little from a rainstorm lasting two hours, but we found no more efficient way of catching it. Later, in quite different weather, we found that we had too much water. We adopted this procedure whenever it rained and, because the rubber coating was gradually washed off the canopy, the water we collected was always tainted and was never really pleasant.

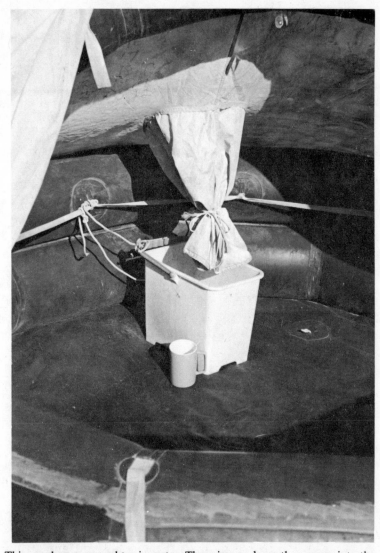

This was how we caught rain water. The rain ran down the canopy into the vent chute and collected in the bucket. It was then baled out with a mug into bottles and containers.

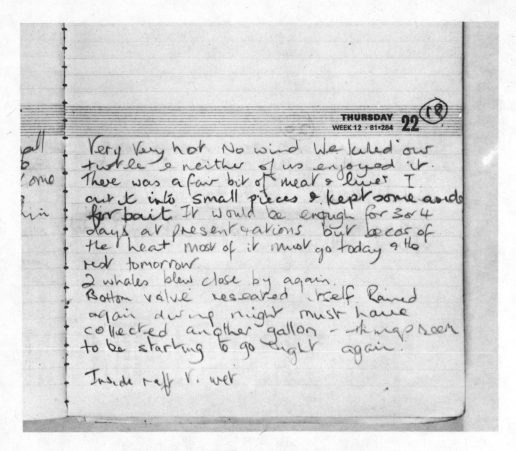

Very Very hot No wind. We killed our
turtle & neither of us enjoyed it.
There was a fair bit of meat & liver I
cut it into small pieces & kept some aside
for bait It would be enough for 3 or 4
days at present rations but becos of
the heat most of it must go today & the
rest tomorrow.
2 whales blew close by again.
Bottom valve reseated itself Rained
again during night must have
collected another gallon — things seem
to be starting to go right again.

Inside reff V. wet

We caught and killed our second turtle. This time we stripped the carcass and ate as much as we could. We took the steaks from its shoulders and pelvic region, and carefully extracted the liver, heart and kidneys.

We also found a large quantity of fat beneath the shell and in other parts of the body. It was greenish yellow in colour and we thought it delicious and appetizing. Once we had tasted the delicate meat we found it very palatable and looked forward with relish to our next turtle. Perhaps it was our bodies crying out for a particular nourishment that made us crave for more.

Before our next turtle, we had a series of rainstorms. It rained for so long that we were able to collect enough water not

72

only to fill all our empty containers, but also to replace some of our original water which had become tainted through exposure to the sun. When the rain came it would last for several hours, keeping us busy collecting the water in our bucket and transferring it cup by cup to the containers, and mopping up continuously to keep the floor as dry as possible. Despite all our efforts the contents of the raft became thoroughly wet. With very little rest we became very tired, which only deepened our depression.

March 26th
(22) We settled down to our night routine of regular watches and an awesome silence settled over our world. I took the first watch. Rarely in our lives had we been able to spend so much of our time gazing at the sky. I looked in wonder at the immensity and clarity of the curtain of stars above me. It was a moment of peace.

The unfamiliar equatorial night sky bewildered me. There was Sirius and Rigel and Capella, but which was Pollux and Kochab? They were lost in the multitude of shining objects, a view unspoilt by any accumulation of haze or cloud. Stretching unobstructed in every direction the boundless sky pivoted slowly around me.

I flashed the torch at my watch. Already it was time to change over, but it seemed a pity to wake Maralyn. I sat a little longer and looked at the sky and watched the meteorites hurry beneath the stars only to burn up in an unexpected moment.

From my meditations came clear resolutions for the future; resolutions that would affect my entire attitude to people. I was conscientiously determined, I told myself, to listen to people's arguments with patience and compassion. Intolerance, although not always a bad thing, must never again colour my criticism. I resolved to improve my selfish approach to our endeavours; to reduce my ego to equable proportions.

It was time to wake Maralyn.

Maralyn

Although we were eating a fair amount of fish I noticed Maurice getting thinner almost day by day, his ribs showed plainly and his cheeks were becoming more sunken. His whole face had a gaunt appearance which was not helped by his rapidly growing beard. We were also losing our sun tan as we kept out of the sun as much as possible. It was hard to imagine that less than three weeks ago we had been fit and tanned, yet now we were pale and emaciated.

When we started out from Panama we had no excess fat and we weighed 118 pounds and 158 pounds respectively. We seemed to lose weight rapidly during the first month and afterwards the rate slowed down. We did not have a mirror, but after much persistent questioning, Maurice told me that my face looked very gaunt. The bruise I had received on my cheekbone had disappeared, but my shins were still bruised and tender from the knocks I had received when leaving the yacht. Our limbs seemed wasted and I thought that our leg muscles probably would not support us for very long.

Water was the main problem at first as we had little rain and it was very hot. Our lips became dry and cracked and the small sips we allowed ourselves from our water flask didn't seem to help very much. Fortunately, we ate fish which helped to alleviate our thirst, but we were getting tired of our fish diet and longed for another turtle to pass by. We had dreamt of the steaks we obtained from the last turtle and they gradually became more and more desirable. We had thought that raw fish would be more palatable than raw turtle meat, but the more fish we ate the less enthusiasm we had for it.

March 28th (24) When the next medium-sized female turtle did come along we had none of our previous hesitation. I quickly pushed my head through the vent and, seeing the turtle immediately below me, I caught one of its rear flippers. Maurice, who had in the meantime got into the dinghy, paddled round and, taking hold of the other flipper, he hauled it into the dinghy in record time. We followed the same procedure but this time after taking off the steaks and exposing the intestines

we decided to explore further. We found a large heart and
took that out and kept it on one side. We then discovered
a large liver which occupied one quarter of the carapace. It
took both of us many minutes of careful concentration to
remove it as it was very slippery and we knew the importance
of getting it out without breaking the green sac. The gall
bladder is full of bitter liquid which contaminates the rest
of the meat if it bursts.

We decided to remove all the intestines. I cut through the
gullet while Maurice severed the restricting membranes and
fed the packed tubes over the side. As the intestines unwound
and trailed in the sea we gazed with amazement at the contents
—they were packed with pieces of crab shell. Perhaps this
was why they were attracted to the raft. Maybe they came for
small crabs which had taken up residence beneath us.

When all the intestines had gone we held the shell over the
side for a few seconds to wash away the blood and when we
brought it back on board we continued with our exploration.
I found several small but extremely tender steaks above the
pelvic bones. Then attached to the shell I found two large
kidneys which were almost round in shape, very pale and
divided into innumerable small segments which reminded me
of a pomegranate. We each started nibbling them and found
them crunchy but they had too much membrane. Nothing
else of interest was found in this turtle; there were no eggs.

We ate a small part of the liver but I found it too sweet and
sickly. Most of it we threw overboard because it was no good
as fish bait since it slipped off the hook too easily. We tried the
heart and found it much more palatable, but rejected the
membrane.

I washed the steaks several times in sea water and cut them
into thin strips. That evening we ate them with half a tin of
bolognaise sauce, each strip being dipped in the sauce. It gave
me a feeling that it wasn't quite so uncivilized to eat it in this
way.

When we killed a turtle the fish seemed to be over-excited
with blood and titbits and became very careless or maybe
over-confident. They even grabbed a blood-sodden plastic

March 28th
(24)
sponge when it was washed in the sea. Several other varieties began to take the hook including some 'silver fish' which were more streamlined, a beautiful grey-silver colour with a lilac 'V' on the side of their head which disappeared when it came out of the water. They were about nine inches long and extremely tender. It was always a special treat to catch one.

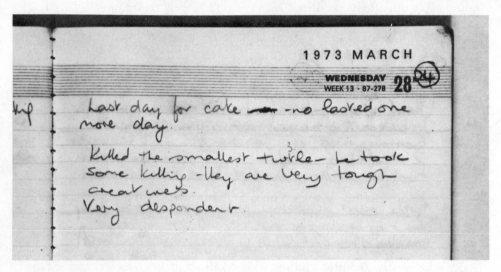

1973 MARCH

WEDNESDAY 28
WEEK 13 · 87-278

trip — Last day for cake — no lasted one more day.

Killed the smallest turtle — he took some killing — they are very tough creatures.

Very despondent.

Maurice

March 29th
(25)
Fourth turtle

When we caught this turtle, a medium-sized female and hauled it into the dinghy, it fought violently as we tried to lay it on its back. The beautiful well-formed creature flayed the air with its flippers and the solitary claws caught our legs and bodies causing some nasty scratches. It was never still; though upside down, it propelled itself round with its flippers by pushing on the dinghy sides. The snapping, toothless jaws caught everything they passed. For the first time we feared for the safety of the dinghy; it just might be possible for its jaws to penetrate the fabric.

I tried to control the reptile by catching its front flippers and its strength astonished me. We would have to kill this one straight away, I thought angrily, and I told Maralyn so. My awkward, unbalanced position of bending over the turtle made

76

me move my feet to a more suitable position. Immediately the turtle caught my right ankle in its powerful jaws. It bit painfully into the loose skin and held on.

To release my hold would have allowed its dangerous flippers to strike us. After a moment's hesitation I pulled my ankle away from the turtle's jaw, tearing the skin. I cursed. "Get the knife and cut its throat," I said to Maralyn.

Without delay, Maralyn began the gory business of slaughtering the turtle. She persevered with the exhausting work until the animal had ceased moving. What a mess! Blood had splattered everywhere and a certain amount had also spilled in our attempts to collect it. Now we relaxed, glad to be finished with this most unpleasant task. How brutal life seemed as we examined our unfortunate victim. However, we felt little remorse for its fate. We needed its life-giving meat.

We sat for some little time resting and eating the congealed blood we had managed to collect. We discovered two parasitic crabs sheltering beneath the tail. These we threw over the side and we were surprised to discover that they *swam* for refuge under the raft. Were there then crabs that would swim in the sea? It was curious how often accepted notions collapsed when one lived so close to nature.

Once more we began the task of cutting away the plastron, or lower shell. With only our small penknife suitable for the task we took turns in cutting through the shell and tough hide. It was now a relatively easy task to cut away the steaks as the anatomy of the turtle was more familiar to us. The meat covering the shoulder blades was removed first so that the bones could be lifted to expose the liver. The liver was lifted cautiously out of the corpse. We then cut the heart out.

As we cut as much meat as we could from the pelvic bone, we searched vainly for any eggs, but extracted the two large kidneys found above the bone.

There was an abundance of the greenish fat which we carefully collected. "This meat will have to last us two days," Maralyn said. "If it remains cool it should still be fresh tomorrow." A sensible suggestion as it would save us the irksome business of fishing that night and in the morning.

77

Maralyn

On March 29th we saw our second ship. We had kept a strict watch throughout the night and as I watched the stars during my watch, I saw one move on the northern horizon. That was odd, I thought, and looked again. I held my breath; it can only be a ship.

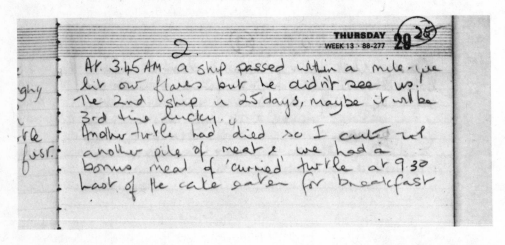

THURSDAY 29
WEEK 13 · 88-277

2.

At 3.45 AM a ship passed within a mile-we lit our flares but he didn't see us! The 2nd ship in 25 days, maybe it will be 3rd time lucky. Another turtle had died so I cut up yet another pile of meat & we had a bonus meal of 'curried' turtle at 9.30 Last of the cake eaten for breakfast

It was 3.45 a.m. I didn't want to wake Maurice and raise his hopes if it turned out to be a false alarm but suddenly as the ship rose above a swell I saw a red navigation light as well as the masthead lights. I shook Maurice awake and collected our two remaining flares. The ship, a tanker, its masthead lights nearly in line came steadily on. We saw the deck lights picking out clearly the ship's structure and the warm glow of light from the portholes as the ship came closer. Maurice took the first flare—a red one. The fates were really against us because that flare was also a dud but we had suffered so many misfortunes that this calamity was taken in our stride. Maurice tossed it into the sea without a word and reached for our last flare.

The second flare worked perfectly and illuminated both raft and dinghy and a large area around us. We felt confident that the watch keepers on the boat would see us. As the flare faded Maurice began flashing SOS with the torch. Relentlessly the ship proceeded on its way until its stern light once more became a bright 'star' on the horizon.

Two ships in twenty-five days; I tried to console Maurice by saying "Third time lucky", but it did little to lift our flagging spirits. As if the weather reflected our mood March came to a close with squally, wet, dismal days. The only good thing about this weather was an ample supply of fresh water.

April 6th
(33)

In the emergency pack I had placed a small sample tube of toothpaste and two toothbrushes, a tablet of soap and a comb. The soap wouldn't create any lather no matter how hard we tried and after a couple of weeks it became so soggy that we threw it into the sea in disgust. The tingly, fresh peppermint taste of toothpaste was wonderful, but somewhat marred by a salt-water rinse.

Maurice combed his hair and beard without difficulty but my long wavy hair became very tangled and it would take

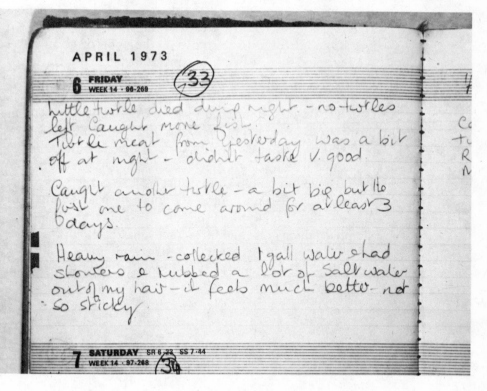

fifteen minutes each morning to comb it carefully out. How often I threatened to cut it off, but resisted! I did trim Maurice's moustache when it began to curl into his mouth and irritate him. I tried washing my hair with salt water but it didn't work too well. It was still lifeless and dull. Later, when we had so much rain that my hair was continually wet, it did become soft and shiny once more.

During the first two weeks of April, squall followed squall. There was no need to restrict ourselves on the amount of water we drank at this time, both fish and turtles were also plentiful. We had only caught the smallest turtles to eat and ignored the larger ones but as so many large ones were around now we decided to tie them to the raft and see if they would tow us.

April 8th
(35)
We caught a large male and held him upside down in the water and put two half-hitches round its rear flippers. To our amazement he towed us in the direction of the Galápagos! They must be incredibly strong swimmers as this one towed us fast enough for us to be able to see the ripple of a bow wave. We reasoned that two or three turtles would tow us faster. It was with great excitement that we caught another large male turtle and harnessed him. I had visions of driving our 'team' right into harbour! The vision was quickly shattered when this turtle began to swim the opposite way! Just our luck to choose one who had no sense of direction. but we left him tethered hoping he would follow the good example of his fellow.

When we turned the large turtles over to harness them, we found sucker fish nestling in the loose flesh under the rear flippers, they usually came in pairs, one under each flipper. We prised them loose and threw them into the dinghy to use as bait. They made excellent fish bait and often instead of capturing and killing a turtle we merely tipped him on end and removed the sucker fish.

"The vision was quickly shattered when this turtle began to swim the opposite way!"

7 The Second Month

Maurice

April 10th
(37)

I was sitting in the dinghy engrossed in the task of fishing. It was a good day and, although the sea was choppy, the sun shone and now it was mid-morning and the fish were biting readily.

Maralyn's exasperated voice entered my thoughts. "A ship, can't you see that ship," she cried from the raft. Startled, I looked around the horizon with an empty gaze.

"Behind you," Maralyn said. Then I saw it—a large freighter sailing East.

Maralyn had been writing and said, "I could hear it from inside the raft." I stared at her in amazement; even now the ship was only one-and-a-half miles away and I could not hear it.

"Your ears are very sensitive," I remarked.

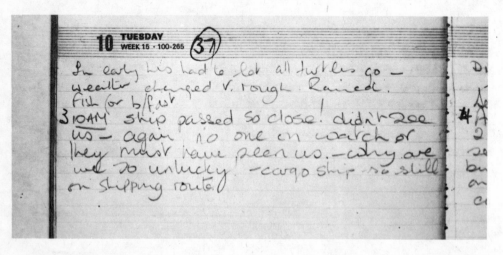

82

Maralyn

We both stared at it in disbelief—it was so close, about half a mile only. We had no flares but waved oilskins. Like the others the ship ploughed a steady course and soon vanished from view. We were both very depressed and couldn't understand why no one had seen us. Were we invisible? I couldn't understand why our luck had deserted us—since 4th March we had had nothing but bad luck, surely it was time for a change of fortune.

We decided to prepare for the next ship and make some flares. As I left *Auralyn* I had grabbed some clothes and their hangers from the wardrobe. I now removed the hook from the hanger and tearing some shirts into strips we wound them round and round the hanger, tying each layer separately. We had two wooden and one metal hanger, so we now had three flares. We intended to light them by first soaking them in the kerosene container then pour a little methylated spirits over each to make them ignite quickly and easily.

We also decided to try and make a smoke flare. I had taken my 'birthday' cake from the boat. This was an ordinary Dundee cake which we planned to share with friends in the Marquesas Islands on my birthday, April 24th. We had carefully cut the cake into sixteen wedges and ate one slice each for breakfast. Unfortunately, it was now finished and the empty tin became the basis of our 'smoke flare'. We collected scraps of cloth and tore pages from the books and made them into tight screws. We hoped that by dampening down the fire it would emit smoke.

At 3.30 p.m., two days later we had the opportunity to put our plans into action.

Maurice

We sat quietly in the raft during the afternoon. Maralyn suddenly tensed, got to her knees and crawled quickly for the door. "I can hear a ship," she said.

April 12th
(39)

83

The fourth ship   Although I could not hear it I joined her and together we peered out into the bright sunlit sea. The waves were choppy and the sun, just on our latitude, therefore spending most of the afternoon in the west, was now sinking towards the horizon. The trade wind sky was laid out in streets of cumulus clouds, driven along by a fresh south-east wind.

Now I could hear the dull and distant roar of powerful diesel engines. My eyes, squinting in the sun, failed to pick out the ship and yet, she was there somewhere.

"There it is," Maralyn called. "Over there."

84

"It's stopping," Maralyn called. "Now it's turning."

I looked in the direction she was pointing and I saw a small white ship, often lost in the ocean swell, approaching from the north. The ship's course must have been nearly due south.

"This one will pass us very close," I said. "I must get into the dinghy and try and make some smoke. You start waving your jacket."

Maurice makes a bonfire
I collected the matches, the cake tin, some rags and my jacket, and scrambled into the dinghy. Maralyn was already waving her jacket enthusiastically. I tore up the rags and packed them into the cake tin, then I poured kerosene and some methylated spirit into the tin.

Then I placed the tin into an empty turtle shell for safety.

I struck a match, and lit the bonfire and held the turtle shell aloft. Fanned by the wind, the flames leapt up from the tin. The small amount of smoke given off from the blazing tin was disappointing. I placed the bonfire at my feet and reaching quickly for a wet towel, began to dampen the flames, hoping that the resulting smoke would be an improvement.

85

Again I held the tin high and smoke billowed from the smouldering rags. Although it was being driven almost horizontal by the wind, we thought that there would be enough smoke to indicate our position.

"It's stopping," Maralyn called, commenting on the ship's movement. "Now it's turning."

The ship, a quasi-military looking vessel, had indeed stopped and we watched spellbound as it began to turn. It was difficult for us to judge at first which way the ship was turning, but eventually we discerned that it was her bows that were slowly moving away from us. It was so close. It could not be farther than half a mile. They must have seen us. . . .

We could not take our eyes off the ship as its bows, and starboard side appeared again. It had turned 180 degrees. Excitedly we began to anticipate the ship's approach. How I wished that I had included a heliograph in my emergency pack.

The ship stood still for some minutes. Tirelessly Maralyn continued to wave; my smoke had nearly finished and I began to wave my jacket.

The ship began moving, turning away from us, and within a very short time had completed another 180 degree turn. Then it sat motionless, its waterline disappearing in the troughs of the waves and swell.

"Come on, don't keep us waiting," I called. My arm ached with waving my jacket. "All right, don't come then," I shouted. "We'll wait for the next one." As if responding to my shouts, the ship started to move forwards on its course to the south. It steamed on oblivious to our signals. It was soon out of sight.

"How could they have not seen us?" asked Maralyn, unable to keep her grief from her voice.

"They probably did see us—to start with—then they must have lost us in the waves and failed to spot us again. Don't forget, we were directly in line with the sun. It would have been very difficult for them," I said miserably, unsure that I would ever regain the spirit to carry on. *Two ships in two days*. Would there be no change to our luck?

86

This photograph was taken in the English Channel on a fairly smooth day when there was little swell. The raft and dinghy were about 500 yards from the camera. It is surprising how difficult it is to pick them out close to the horizon and slightly left of centre. Some of the ships passed within about 800 or 900 yards of the raft when it was in the Pacific, but there was a considerable swell, and conditions were often very much rougher.

87

It was then that Maralyn's true attitude towards religion
occurred to me. I had previously thought that she shared
with me similar sceptical views.

My own atheism took root, I think, in my youth when no
adult had been able to satisfy my doubts. It was as though I
had to accept religious tradition without question, much as
one would accept distorted history as portrayed by some
romantic writer. I rebelled, I suppose, as only the young can
rebel and became impatient with the unthinking approval
given to this dead tradition. It was hard to equate my world of
man's practical genius with the superstition generated by the
religious. My world, as I saw it, was real. There was no
"world for little children" and my teachers, perhaps unintentionally, drove thoughts of a practical religion from my
mind. They taught dogmatic theories; my education became
a deceitful sham.

Maralyn, I found, was really a fatalist. She believed that
much of what happened to us and what we did was pre-
destined. Her explanation of the ordeal we were undergoing
was that it was preparing us for things in the future. There
must be a reason why we had survived so long, she explained.
Perhaps her world was, in fact, governed by a supreme being
although, like many people, she was reluctant to call it God.
She had no fear of a deity.

In any case, Maralyn had little time for orthodox religion
and, like me, tended to be intolerant of clerics. Looking back,
I tried to find some clue to her confidence and vigour. Then
I remembered an earlier incident as we lay at anchor in
Antigua in the West Indies, when she said softly and thought-
fully, "I don't want to go on."

I felt exasperated, "Why, the trip has been marvellous and
nothing has gone wrong. We're fitter than we have ever been
and the prospect of visiting the South Pacific islands is
exciting."

"Yes, but I would like to return to England and build
another, larger boat," Maralyn said. "I would like to sail
next time with June and Colin and show them all the marvellous places we have visited."

"Don't forget the English climate and how it affected your arthritis," I said, "and what about our prospects of finding a well-paid job straight away."

"I know," said Maralyn, "but I have a certain feeling that we ought to go back now and build what we have learned into another boat."

She was not insistent and the matter passed and I did not think of it again until that moment. Had she, however, had some premonition of disaster? It might just be coincidence, but now, although depressed at times, her confidence in our ultimate survival remained undimmed. Her faith in some supernatural power governing our affairs never weakened.

Lightheartedly, in an effort to bolster my flagging spirits, she forecast the ship that would rescue us. It was to be, she told me, a large, black Russian container-ship steaming east towards Panama. That it eventually turned out to be a small, white Korean fishing boat sailing west, did not cause her to repent in the very least.

Maralyn

There followed a few days of rough weather which did nothing to lighten our low spirits. We were tossed and bounced around like a rubber ball, we just hoped that the seas would calm down before another ship appeared as it would have been difficult to be seen in the large swells.

> **17 TUESDAY** WEEK 16 · 107-258 Jewish Passover (414)
> Not very bright this morning
> Both have jubbly tums & diarrhœa.
> Cooler. overcast & v. lumpy
> Weather miserable —like us Depressed.

Our watch keeping was not so strict now, as we were both extremely tired and found it difficult to stay awake during the night.

Around 8 p.m. I would shuffle down for a rest and with my feet under Maurice's arm, I could rest my head on the top tube of the raft and in this half-reclining position I would doze until midnight. We then changed places and I sat by the door while Maurice tried to get some sleep. We tried to maintain watch but invariably the person on watch also began to doze after half an hour or so. We both realized it was impossible to keep an alert watch and accepted the situation.

At the changeover of watch at midnight another ship passed. The sea had not gone down and a considerable swell was running. With great difficulty Maurice hauled the dinghy close to the raft and choosing his moment carefully, flopped into the dinghy, I tied the two craft together and handed Maurice one of the home-made flares. He dipped it into our kerosene container and when he decided it was sufficiently soaked, held it towards me. I poured methylated spirits over it and applied a match. Nothing happened. I tried again and again. The wind was strong but even when I shielded the match the flare would not light. Time was passing. "It's no good, try the torch," I gasped. I handed Maurice the torch knowing it would be a miracle if anyone picked out the pin prick of light which it gave out. The batteries were almost finished and only a pale yellow light flickered from the torch. Unaware of our plight the ship moved across our line of vision. Portholes passed by, each brightly illuminated betraying the fact that there was human life on board. We saw no movement and no person. She passed out of sight and on into the black void.

Despair and exhaustion took over. In silence we settled back into the raft and resumed the same positions. We began to feel that ships disturbed our peace. If they weren't going to stop we didn't want to see them.

Next morning we found our kerosene container had become a mixture of oil and water, in fact, mostly water, therefore useless. We emptied the liquid away and left the container without the lid to let the smell escape. We also threw the small

April 19th (46) container of methylated spirits into the dinghy and abandoned the idea of using flares. This may seem to indicate that we were resigned to our fate, but fate also took a hand a few days later when we discovered our matches damp and beyond resuscitation. Although I spent many hours spreading them out in the sun, when we tried to strike them the heads fell off.

Before the sun rose Maurice baled out the dinghy and put our pet turtle over the side for a swim. We had named him Rastus and had caught him fourteen days ago. He was only small, about two feet long, and was secured to the dinghy by a rope in the usual manner with two half hitches around his rear flipper. Each morning Maurice put him over the side and he swam while we fished. He always swam in the direction of the Galápagos Islands. He was then brought back on board, placed in the front of the dinghy, and covered with wet rags during the heat of the day. Usually he had another swim during our evening fishing session, but occasionally he just levered himself half on to the dinghy thwart and watched the proceedings with a sorrowful eye.

April 20th (47) Next morning, Maurice went across to the dinghy at dawn and discovered that Rastus was dead. We both felt sorry for the unfortunate creature as indeed he had come to be loved as a pet. He had been our reserve food supply for fifteen days and now the time had come for us to eat him.

We were certainly now in an east-going current, which we found warmer than the chilling Humboldt. Maurice estimated that our drift with the aid of our sail might be as much as twenty to twenty-five miles a day to the north-east. If only we could rely on this current, and the predominantly southerly winds, we could possibly reach the American coast in about twenty days. We fondly imagined that our luck would hold; that from now on the currents and winds would remain favourable.

Each day we followed the same routine and worked before the sun rose too high. After helping Maurice fish I would return to the raft with our breakfast, top up the raft with air and make sure everything was tidy. When Maurice had cleaned the dinghy he would join me for breakfast. We ate slowly, the meal usually lasting for an hour. After I had washed up and cleared away we would dream and doze away the day until our evening fishing time.

Occasionally we still played cards and dominoes but more often we read our two books and occasionally played a word game. We talked of our life before and during the voyage and what it would be like afterwards.

How often I would lean on the edge of the raft dreamily gazing at the multi-coloured aquarium swimming lazily below me. A sleek white two-masted sailing boat sailed across my mind's eye, a thing of beauty, yet purposeful. I walked the decks and peeped below into the various cabins noting the furnishings and the varnished woodwork. How could I persuade Maurice that I longed for another yacht just like this dream ship.

For so many years we had planned our life afloat, we couldn't give up now. It was the life we had chosen, the life Maurice was happy with. Yet he was now prepared to give up this life, swallow the anchor, and return to the life he had found so restricting, because he was convinced I would no longer wish to sail. He spoke of the house we would buy, with a large garden for me to potter around in and grow all our vegetables once more, and fill the flowerbeds with a riot of colour. Although I talked with enthusiasm I knew that, peaceful as this plan sounded, it was not really what either of us wanted. For a short time it would have been relaxing but deep down within us both was the restless urge to travel 'beyond the sunset', a desire to see strange places, different people, and animals in their natural surroundings. We had to go on.

As Maurice stirred I gathered my thoughts together and decided to tell him of the dream ship and the voyages we would make in her. Once I had persuaded him I still loved the sea

92

Thinking about our new yacht, *Auralyn II*, helped us to keep up our morale.
We filled several pages of the Log Book and the Diary with sketches and notes.

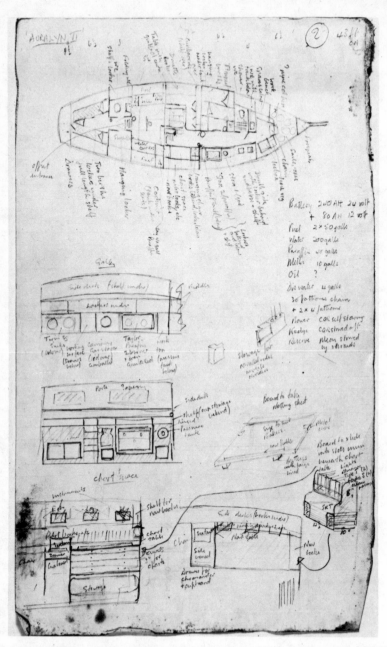

Accommodation details for *Auralyn II*.

Auralyn II and ships, we both found an enormous amount of pleasure designing our next yacht and home. We planned to live aboard again as we had done with *Auralyn*.

Hour after hour passed as we discussed our plans down to each minute detail. Maurice drew the outline of the yacht and gradually we filled it out as we decided on the layout. Each section was itemized and I wrote down all the details in our log book. Once we had designed the boat I spent days planning a provision list and stocking the boat for an extended voyage, and when we had decided on the quantity of food we spent a long time discussing its stowage, and the positioning of locker space. These preparations ran into weeks; in fact we had two favourite subjects—our yacht and food.

I had read that people starving think of very little except food, and to a large extent this is true. We talked of holidays, but the place and journey were the minor part; the food we would eat on this holiday took the major part. Entertaining on our new yacht was a fascinating topic. Not only did I plan out menus, but discussed how each item should be cooked and in what order. Maurice learnt more about cooking in theory than he had ever done in practice.

April 24th Maralyn's birthday The day began fine, but dull; the seas were much calmer but lumpy. It was my birthday. As a special treat Maurice started fishing early and kept trying for a large silver milk-fish whose flesh we particularly liked, but he found it a difficult task to catch one with our barbless hooks. We both got excited as time and time again the fish took the bait—but not the hook. It was getting over-confident however and we recognized the signs—soon it would make a mistake.

"I've got it!" yelled Maurice as he struggled with the line. I kept my fingers crossed as I had seen this happen so many times before. The hook was not strong enough to take the weight of such a large fish, and they usually escaped when almost within reach. This time was no exception—within inches of the dinghy it gave a vicious tug and pulled free of the hook; like a catapult the hook flicked back, and to our horror embedded itself in the dinghy.

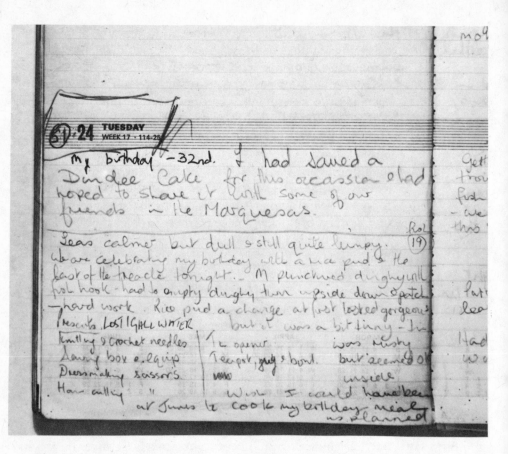

The dinghy is punctured

Automatically Maurice pulled it out and a slow hiss started. Bubbles popped on the surface of the sea as air escaped from the punctured tube. As the puncture was just under water, we knew we would have to lift the dinghy clear to patch it. I took some of the water carriers from Maurice and placed them in the raft, and the rest were floated and tied to the outside. Maurice then returned to the raft and we both knelt in the doorway and lifted the side of the dinghy, resting it on the top tube of the raft. We only had the repair kit which was supplied with the raft and as we read through the instructions, we realized that if we had only had one craft it would have been impossible to repair any leak near the water, and this was the most vulnerable place.

96

April 24th
(51)
Following the instructions carefully, we dried and cleaned the appropriate area and applied the first coat of glue. We had to wait until this was dry and already my arms began to ache with holding the dinghy in place, but I could not let go as it would get wet. Maurice took over for a while to give me some relief. When the glue was dry, I took hold of the dinghy again while Maurice applied the second coat of glue and then, carefully, a small round patch. We both held on to the dinghy until it was perfectly dry and then surveyed our handiwork. Although it had been an effort in our weakened state, we were pleased with it, and resolved to be more careful with fish hooks in future.

We returned the dinghy to the sea and reloaded it. I noticed Maurice looking puzzled and enquired what the matter was.

"I'm sure we had more water containers," he said.

"Are you sure you've counted properly?"

"Well you count and see if I'm right."

I counted, then counted again. He was right, one container had disappeared! We scanned the sea around us, but could see no trace of our water carrier. Our feeling of achievement rapidly dissolved as we realized the cost of one small patch was four days' water supply. To try and raise our spirits I reminded Maurice that today *was* my birthday, and tonight we would celebrate.

That night we opened and shared out our one and only rice pudding topped with the remains of the treacle. It was thick, creamy and wonderful, and we ate it in blissful silence. Afterwards we came back to reality and agreed that it had tasted a bit tinny; the tin was very rusty, but it seemed we had caught it in time, although had we kept it for much longer I think it would have 'blown'.

April 25th
(52)
Next morning was calm again, but as we fished we noticed that our drogue was missing. We examined the lines which appeared to have been cleanly cut. I suppose some fish, or maybe a turtle, must have snapped through them. But the weather was calmer, and we were drifting slowly, so a drogue was not of major importance at that time. We returned to our

97

April 26th
(53)

fishing, keeping a careful eye on the hook and continually reminding each other of yesterday's catastrophe. The round black patch on the grey dinghy was a conspicuous reminder, and inevitably our eyes riveted on this spot.

The repair
fails

Early next morning I was gazing at the dinghy and realized I could not see the black spot. I tried to convince myself it was all right, because the patch was on the other side. I lay there, going over the patching operation and was convinced I was looking at the right side.

When Maurice woke up, I quizzed him as to which side of the dinghy he had patched? After a thoughtful minute he replied "Port side."

"That's what I thought and if we're both right the patch has gone."

An examination of the dinghy did prove us both right—the patch had floated away. Fortunately some of the glue seemed to have blocked the hole a little and reduced the leak, but from then on we had to pump the dinghy at least twice a day.

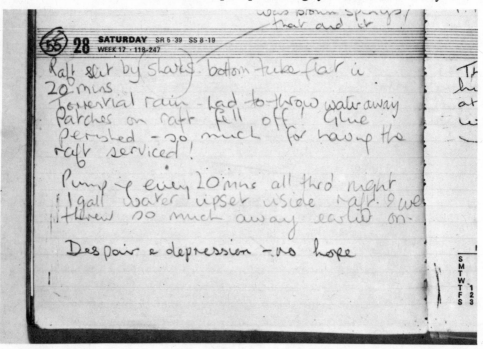

The spine-
foot

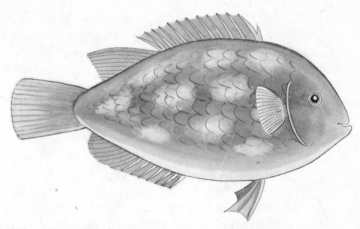

Spinefoot. Ten to fifteen inches long. Brown and white mottled appearance. Rather stupid looking. Flesh very tender.

April 28th
The raft is
punctured

As if to continue our current run of bad luck, two days; later the raft was punctured. During the night the raft always became soft, probably because of the change in temperature, but on this particular morning we awoke to find the bottom tube completely flat. We fitted up the pump, but after thirty or forty pumps nothing happened, and we realized it must be punctured. But where? We carried on pumping and after another thirty pumps it appeared to be half-inflated. Maurice clambered into the dinghy and told me to keep pumping while he searched for the leak. It didn't take long to find—by the doorway on the starboard side were a row of tiny holes.

Large mottled brown spinefoot fish had been keeping us company for several weeks; they seemed to arrive with a turtle but would then transfer their allegiance to the raft. These fish had a number of large, strong spines running the length of their backs. It was not a very adventurous fish; occasionally it did come forth and nibble at the bait but usually hovered in the shade under the raft. We reasoned that it must have been surprised by some predator whilst it was sheltering and had raised its spines in defence, and in the process had punctured us.

Mechanically we went through the routine of patching the puncture. In view of our previous experience we were not very

confident of success. This time the patch didn't even adhere
but lifted off as soon as we dropped the raft back in the water.
The task had exhausted us physically and mentally. Would
the raft be so stable now that its freeboard had been reduced
by the deflated lower tube? Would it last much longer? But
it had to; without its canopy we could not stand the intolerable heat of the relentless sun.

Not having fished that morning we sat through the rest of
the day nursing our sorrows and tried to cheer ourselves by
eating a 'morale booster'. We had rescued a large tin of
treacle and two tins of condensed milk. The treacle had been
finished and now we broached the last of our condensed milk.
The glutinous, sweet milk had the desired effect and gradually
we could discuss our situation logically and by sundown had
come to the conclusion that we must learn to live with our
floppy raft. The only daunting feature was the regularity
with which we needed to pump it up. Our weight made
everything sag towards the centre and restricted our living
space, but the worst feature was the 'pinching' from the
rubberized material. As the floor sagged and creased, the
movement of the water beneath us made it writhe and squirm
as if it were alive. The continual movement chafed and pinched
what little flesh we had left on our bones, and from this day
until our rescue we never found a comfortable position in the
raft for more than five minutes at a time.

To keep the floor reasonably firm we had to pump every
15 to 20 minutes. We found this impossible to keep up during
the nights that followed and only pumped up every 30 or 40
minutes, or when we could no longer stand the acute discomfort. Often we would both fall asleep from sheer exhaustion and awake to find the raft so flat that we were held captive
in the folds of the material. As we pumped it back into shape
the luxury was wonderful and our spirits rose. "If only it
would stay like this," I said, "raft life might even become
tolerable."

Maurice

As the days progressed, we became shocked at the physical decline in each other. Maralyn's brown, smooth skinned and supple body had now developed into a thin bony frame motivated by stiff and sore limbs. Her sunken eyes accentuated the gauntness of her face.

My beard, to a large extent, must have disguised the drawn and angular features of my face but I could feel the bones as they protruded through my skin. Our muscles were slack and wasted.

Our emaciated state horrified us. There was all this natural food around us and yet we were not, apparently, getting sufficient nourishment.

Day followed day without making any impact on our minds. We could make no true distinction between different days of the week. Only the change from day to night and the fluctuation of the sun's declination, proclaiming the changing seasons, were obvious to us. The passage of the days was noted by Maralyn in her diary. She also faithfully marked each day on the inside of the raft's canopy, putting a circle round family birthdays, whilst turtle days had a cross and ship days a plus sign. We could thus work out the average time between events: four-and-a-half days between turtles, eleven days between ships.

Maralyn supplemented her diary by starting a letter to her friend June in England. She always seemed to be writing. There were times when the diary and her papers would become wet. Then, with infinite care and patience, she would dry them out whenever the sun shone.

As more of the area of the canopy was taken up with Maralyn's markings, the reality of our plight depressed us. The world around us was indeed our own; it was no longer inhabited by humans, only sea creatures. Now only our own endeavours could save us.

Our discussions would sometimes revolve round the probable outcome of our misadventure. It was impossible to say that we viewed our seemingly inevitable death with fear, but more correctly, with resignation. We would occasionally

101

think of what we would do when the end was near, and by
what means we could quickly die. The gas bottle was empty
and suffocation by any other means we thought would be
ineffective. Maralyn did not care for the idea of swimming
away from the raft.

That left only the knife. I did wonder if nature would settle
it for us by sending a poisonous fish into our shoal.

These discussions were fortunately short-lived for Maralyn
never lost hope in our survival. She would frequently boost
my morale by talking about the food she would cook when
we arrived back in England. She had that essential gift of
leadership and showed by her own example the will-power
needed to keep life going.

The passing of the days was also marked on the raft's canopy. A circle
represents a birthday, a turtle day had a cross, and a ship day a plus sign.
We used the felt pen for this.

102

8 The Third Month

Maralyn

Early May   We had been adrift for two months and May brought bad weather. The nylon canopy on our small floating home, having lost its rubber coating and bleached almost white by the sun, was no longer waterproof and each time it rained the whole of the inside became thoroughly sodden. Because of the punctured tube we were that much nearer the water, and waves which normally wouldn't have bothered us, now lapped over the top and into the raft. Sometimes, even on fine days, we were wet through with sea water. We had to bale continuously.

I noticed a split about ten inches long in the tape joining the two circular tubes at the front of the life-raft. The cotton tape had deteriorated in the sun and was now allowing sea water to slop into the raft. This was bad but hardly surprising, the raft having withstood a lot of punishment. If the tape continued to split round the circumference the two tubes would part and we would then have to abandon the raft. It became obvious now that we must be extremely careful and restrict our movements in the raft to a minimum in order to relieve the stresses on the tape.

May also brought bad health. Some of the water had been stored in a white polythene container and had turned very green through the effects of sunlight on it. Not being prepared to throw it away we each drank a cupful. A few hours later we both had violent pains and a mild attack of dysentery. We resolved not to drink any more 'bad water' and, when it rained, to throw it away and replace it with fresh. This incident made us decide to check the rest of the water

We are at our lowest ebb
containers. With horror we discovered that all our water was undrinkable except the two one-gallon containers kept inside the raft.

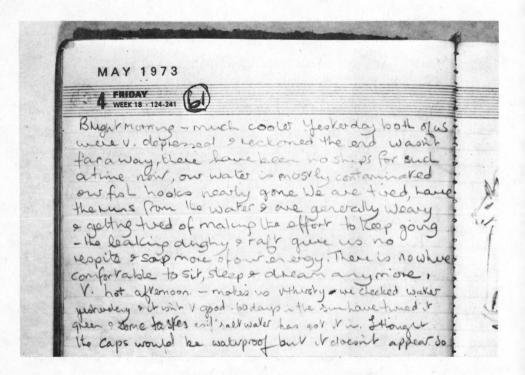

MAY 1973

4 FRIDAY WEEK 18 · 124-241

Bright morning — much cooler. Yesterday both of us were v. depressed & reckoned the end wasn't far away, there have been no ships for such a time now, our water is mostly contaminated our fish hooks nearly gone. We are tired, have the runs from the water & are generally weary & getting tired of making the effort to keep going - the leaking dinghy & raft give us no respite & sap more of our energy. There is no where comfortable to sit, sleep & dream anymore.
V. hot afternoon — makes us v thirsty — we checked water yesterday & it isn't v good - 10 days in the sun have turned it green & some tastes evil, salt water has got v in. I thought the caps would be waterproof but it doesn't appear so.

That same day we managed to catch, on our make-shift bent-pin hooks, two very large milk-fish. We had to watch very carefully and, as soon as they took the bait, yank them into the dinghy before they slipped off the unbarbed hook or caused it to straighten out. After gutting and cleaning we decided to conserve our energy by eating one that morning and having one later for our evening meal, so we would not have to fish again that day. By evening our supper was not as fresh as it should have been and although I could only eat half

104

my share I was violently sick the rest of the night. Maurice did not seem to be affected as much as I was, although he complained of pains and had a slight fever.

I was ill and depressed and was tired of making the effort to sustain life, but I didn't want to die, there was so much to do and see. We had survived sixty days and I reasoned there was some significance in this.

I have never followed any religion and the isolation and insecurity did not bring any form of conversion. I have a strong belief in destiny, fate, kismet, call it what you will. I believe that each happening in our lives prepares us for some eventual test. I also think we have the ability to write our own future. If we want something badly enough, through sheer determination often that goal is achieved. I didn't want to die and I was doing everything in my power to make sure I lived. I had planned out a new life, with a new yacht and arranged in minute detail another epic voyage and I firmly believed I would live to carry out this plan.

As week followed week I became more convinced of this. In normal conditions, when would we have found time to sit and talk for days on end about nothing but the interior of a new boat? Because we had no outside intrusion into our thoughts our concentration was never diverted, consequently the subject was discussed thoroughly.

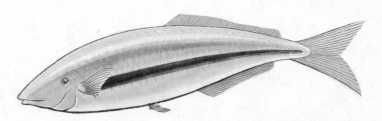

Milk Fish. A Pacific Ocean food fish of great commercial importance. An open sea species which migrates to shallow inshore waters to spawn. Grows up to five feet long. Silver with iridescent blue streak down each side of the body.

105

Probably, never again in the rest of our lives will we have such a period of solitude, devoid of commercial interference. Not only did we plan every aspect of a new boat, but even a list of stores was prepared for our next voyage.

How many people have the opportunity to sit quietly and analyse their feelings for things or each other? We had no secrets, no privacy and no inhibitions. When our morale was low it made us niggardly, and we would say hurtful things to each other. I would cry, regretting it all and we began expressing our apologies. "I would rather serve a prison sentence; at least there would be a known date of release!" I wrote, "Here every day becomes more of a nightmare. If only a ship would see us; it would be unbearable to have another pass us by."

Calmly we could see where we had gone wrong, why we had argued, why we had been intolerant. To begin again was a chance very few people have. In a sense we had died and been reborn, intensely aware of each other and respecting feelings and opinions. We also had confidence in ourselves and our ability to survive any future hardships. We had survived and would continue to survive.

Rolls of thunder heralded the rain. The pitter-patter of rain drops on the canvas revived me like a wilting flower. In the deluge that followed I forgot my depression in the elation I felt as we laboriously replaced gallon after gallon of stagnant water.

Maurice did try fishing but our drift was too fast as we had no sea-anchor. We trailed our bucket which slowed us down but not enough. No fish were caught but just before we gave up for the evening a large male turtle came swimming by. It must have weighed at least 250 pounds and was about three feet, end to end. Maurice took the front flippers and I grabbed the rear. Again and again we tried to lift it clear of the water, each time our efforts were balked by some projection on the dinghy, usually the fixed rowlocks. We strained to lift the reptile until finally Maurice managed to get the turtle's lower shell partly on the tube. Breathless, we rested still holding the turtle as it balanced precariously on the side. With one final

106

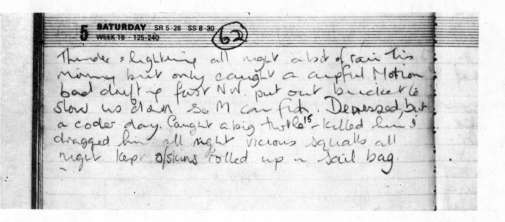

Thunder & lightning all night a lot of rain this morning but only caught a cupful. Motion bad drift ↑ fast N.W. put out bucket to slow us down so M can fish. Depressed, but a coder day. Caught a big turtle[15] - killed him & dragged him all night vicious squalls all night kept o/skins rolled up in sail bag.

Our
fifteenth
turtle
combined effort we heaved it inboard and it lay on its back, its flippers clapping against its shell. It took up most of the floor area of the aft section of the dinghy. It was certainly the largest one we had caught.

As it was getting dusk we decided to kill it but not to eat it until the next day. The wind was increasing and already the sea was building up and so this seemed the best idea. We tied the carcass to the back of the raft and dragged it all night, the body acting as a drogue. Vicious squalls swept over us and although we didn't get much rest we remained quite cheerful, anticipating our breakfast.

May 6th
(63)
The turtle meat was wonderful. We ate the best steaks but if some part was a bit tough or had too much membrane we rejected it and simply said, 'fish bait' as we threw it into a dish. This had become our special phrase for anything that was tough or unpalatable and we came to know that certain steaks taken from the turtle were purely 'fish bait' steaks.

During the spell of rough weather the fish had disappeared, even juicy turtle meat failed to tempt them. We suspected they were swimming deep to avoid the turbulence near the surface. Next morning I saw Maurice eating some of the turtle bait as he was fishing. I told him to stop but it was already too late. He paid for his morning snack with two days of sickness and diarrhoea!

107

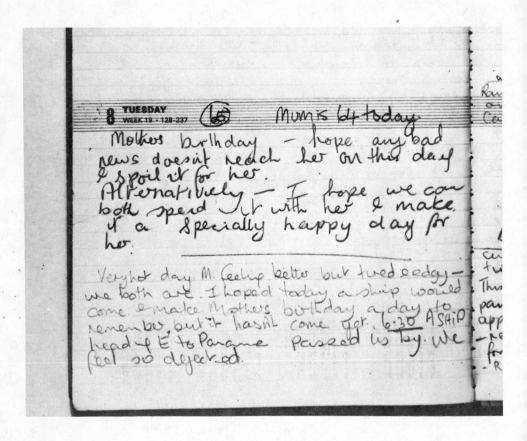

Mum's 64 today

TUESDAY
WEEK 19 · 128-237

Mum's 64 today

Mothers birthday — hope any bad news doesn't reach her on this day & spoil it for her.
Alternatively — I hope we can both spend it with her & make it a specially happy day for her.

Very hot day M. feeling better but tired & edgy — we both are. I hoped today a ship would come & make Mothers birthday a day to remember, but it hasn't come yet. 6.30 A SHIP head up E to Panama passed us by. We feel so dejected.

The sixth ship

May 8th was my mother's birthday and the day dawned bright and clear with the sea calmer than it had been for a good while. The ideal day for a ship to come by. That evening at 6.30 a cargo ship, the sixth we had sighted, passed without seeing us, heading towards Panama. Number seven is supposed to have lucky or significant connections; we felt we could last another two weeks for that ship to come.

Days dragged by and it rained so often that I couldn't remember the last time the inside of the raft had been dry. Maurice began to develop a dry hacking cough which we did not pay much attention to at the time. I would not have been surprised if both of us had caught pneumonia. It was cold, wet and miserable although we did catch enough food to sustain us through that depressing time. After ten weary days the seventh ship came and went. When the initial disappointment had passed we forgot about the ship and resumed our routine of existing amongst our sea creatures.

Auralyn seemed a far and distant dream, an event of a previous life, a fading memory. Our present survival was all consuming and I felt we had always lived like this. Our world shrank to slender proportions and we were upset when our routine was disturbed by intruders.

In some weird and detached way we found peace in our complete and compulsory isolation. We talked without the encumbrances of modern living; we explored the hidden depths of each other's character, we threw away the trappings of so called civilization and reverted to a simple prehistoric way of life. We had our 'lair', the raft, and only emerged to hunt our food. Life was simple, but not secure.

Maurice

It was nearly noon and we rested in the raft. For the first time for many weeks we found bliss in the release from the heavy rain; we revelled in the hot sun as it sent its rays on to our strained and tormented craft.

We both felt physically better. We had dragged ourselves up, temporarily, from the apathy of resignation and we talked together in lively dialogue. However hard we tried, the topic would invariably come back to food. Food in its cultivation, food in its preparation and food in its eating. It was our world of fantasy and in the dubious security of the raft our environment no longer appeared hostile.

I gazed out of the entrance into the clear blue sea, the waves reflecting back the sunlight like a collection of priceless jewels. Screwing up my eyes in the glare I saw a large cargo ship with a blue painted hull within one and a half miles of us. Momentarily I pictured the life on board that freighter. Human life of seamen going to their mid-day meal, of some-one on the bridge preparing to take a noon sight . . . Hell, I thought, if he scans the horizon with a sextant he might just see us!

"There's a ship out there," I said calmly as I scrambled up to my knees.

Maralyn did not speak but collected our oilskins and passed them out to me in the dinghy. Our reactions had become automatic. We waved our arms until they ached, yet there was no enthusiasm in our robot-like movements. The ship steamed steadily on towards Panama and our arm motions became slower. The hull disappeared below the horizon leaving its white superstructure almost invisible in the haze. We stopped waving; it had gone.

"That was the seventh," Maralyn said without emotion.

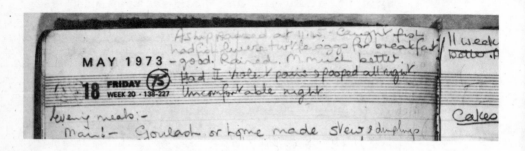

Maralyn

Mid-May This second stage of our strange voyage is difficult to describe. For the next six weeks no ships appeared to interrupt our routine. We felt alone and realized to its full extent the incredible vastness of the ocean. During this time we needed help badly yet no help was forthcoming. We had only each other and had to rely on our own resources.

We had very little leisure time. Fishing, of necessity, became highly organized. Fish fillets in one bowl, skins in another, livers and 'poops' (roes) in a mug and fish eyes in a small tin. We also saved the largest of the fish heads.

Eating our meal also followed a routine. First the skins were scraped of any left-over meat and thrown over the side; next

110

Mid-May the fish heads were split in two and the small amounts of exceptionally sweet meat prised free and eaten. Sometimes we crunched the gills and found them quite palatable although it made us very thirsty. Fish livers were eaten next followed by fillets and fish eyes. A drink of water finished off our meal. Our freshly caught water although tasting of rubber was good and clear, but the water we had stored usually had bits of algae floating in it and we referred to this as our 'oogly' water. It was always a worrying time if we found 'ooglies' in a new batch of

These were the tins and bowls which we used in the dinghy to put the various parts of the fish as we gutted them.

water and we fussed around straining it through a piece of material.

We became very depressed on rough days as we realized there was less chance of us being seen, but a quiet, clear day was always heralded as a 'good ship day'. Often I used to announce a special day. For instance one would be a 'ship day' and another a 'turtle' day; whether or not either turned up was irrelevant.

No ships did steam into our sight and we became so detached that we could joke about this lack of traffic. Towards late afternoon I would say to Maurice, "Well, it doesn't look as if we are going to be invited out for dinner tonight, does it?

An obsession
with food

I suppose we had better do something about preparing our own meal." Long discussions would follow on favourite foods and especially of unusual ways of serving ordinary food. We searched our memories for childhood sweets and foods and realized how much we had relied on prepared and tinned foods. It was many years since either of us had eaten a home-made rice pudding, for instance, or a jam roly-poly. It seemed to be the simple home-made dishes that we craved for.

Our thoughts and conversation became obsessed with food and as we had planned and, in our imagination, built our yacht, we began to live in an imaginary world where we sailed in and out of favourite ports, spoke of restaurants we would revisit, food we would buy and, most of all, discussed meals we would eat on board both at sea and in harbours. We lived in a dream world which had no boundaries beyond the limits of our imagination.

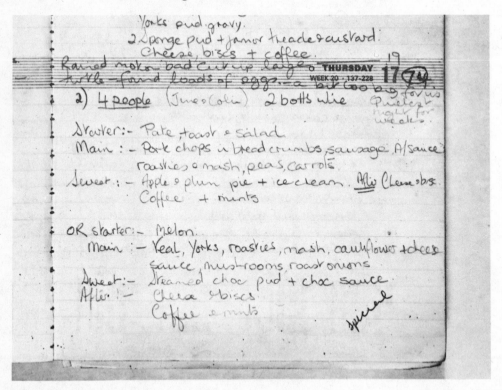

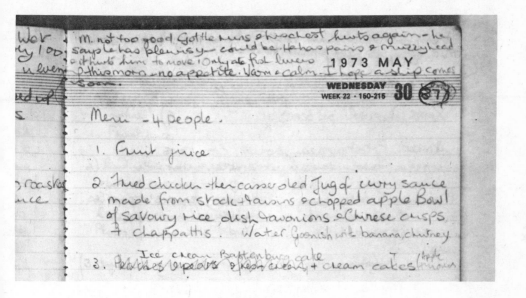

Wot
ly loo
u even
ud up
s
roaskse
nce

M. not too good Got the runs & his chest hurts again - he
sayshe has pleurisy - could be. He has pains & muzzy head
& it hurts him to move. Only ate fish lunes — **1973 MAY**
this morn - no appetite. Warm & calm - I hope a ship comes
soon.

WEDNESDAY
WEEK 22 · 150-215 **30** (87)

Menu - 4 people.

1. Fruit juice

2. Fried chicken - then casseroled. Jug of curry sauce
made from stock + raisins & chopped apple Bowl
of savoury rice dish. Favonions. & Chinese crisps.
+ chappattis. Water Goonish with banana, chutney

3. Peaches & pears & pear cream + cream cakes [nice]
Ice cream Battenburg cake

Maurice becomes ill

Towards the end of May, Maurice became ill. It wasn't a
sudden illness, but seemed to build up over a couple of weeks
until I had to admit something was wrong. Both of us were
very lethargic, but this was not unexpected as we still had
attacks of dysentery, but Maurice complained of pains in his
chest and his cough became more persistent. I said he must
have strained himself pulling a large turtle into the dinghy
and he agreed although I could tell he was not very convinced.
His gaunt face became, if possible, even more pinched and he
had an unhealthy pallor. The day came when he couldn't lift
his arm because of the pain and he was cold and feverish and
said he had a 'muzzy' head. The symptoms reminded him of
an attack of pleurisy he had had many years ago. This was the
last thing we wanted; for one of us to be seriously ill could
be fatal. I did not dare admit my fears about his health; he was
already extremely depressed and the truth would only have
deepened his depression. I chaffed him and encouraged him to
'buck up' and in a way it worked, but he agreed to let me take
over the fishing as he was almost immobile with pain.

113

Maurice

Any movement became intolerable for me, even Maralyn's
encouraging chatter failed to raise my spirits. The ulcerated
sores eating into my flesh were causing a lot of pain. I was
never comfortable. Maralyn soothed the wounds as best she
could with a cosmetic cream.

Chest pains virtually immobilized me and any excessive
movement of my arms only aggravated my distress. A hacking
cough that I had developed interfered with any rest Maralyn
could get and occasionally I coughed up blood. I was taking
very little interest in our survival and Maralyn was bearing an
unfair burden in supplying our food, baling out and inflating
the raft.

"When we get another spell of sunshine, we can dry everything out and you'll begin to feel much better," she said.
"Your sores will be dry and then will soon heal."

I could say nothing, her enthusiasm for life showed in
everything she did and she undertook the butchery of our next
turtle, our twenty-second, by herself. She would not heed my
protest that I *must* help, that she must not treat me like an
invalid.

What was the matter with me? This was no time to develop
any serious illness although, I thought, a little rest might help
recovery.

Maralyn left the raft after making me as comfortable as
possible and started work on the female turtle we had stored
in the dinghy which had, fortunately for her, died during the
night. She worked alone and was, I suppose, as happy as she
could be in the circumstances. It saddened me to think that I
felt too ill to anticipate with any real relish the meat that
Maralyn was cutting up.

"Whoopee," Maralyn cried. "It's full of eggs, try these."
She excitedly passed a dishful of moist, bright golden spheres
each about the size of a large marble. I picked one up; it
was soft like a semi-inflated ball. This did not surprise me
but I had thought of them as having a white covering. At
least, all the illustrations I had seen indicated white eggs.

114

Turtle's
eggs

Turtle's Eggs. A female turtle yields about 150 to 200 eggs. In their un-developed state they are golden-yellow balls of yolk.

These were immature eggs, I supposed, but they were so large that they must have been ready for laying in a week or, at the most, ten days. Turtles are, indeed, powerful swimmers to reach the distant islands to lay the eggs in so short a time.

"There are hundreds," Maralyn said. "Have you tried one yet? They must be full of protein."

I put the egg into my mouth and rolled it around. It had a firm membrane. I burst the membrane and a thick, dry-tasting rich yolk spread over my mouth and throat. It clung in glutinous layers to my teeth and tongue and resisted all efforts of my saliva to wash it away.

"They're good," I said bravely. I ate another, then another. "Too many at once will be rather sickly," I went on. "We shall probably drink more water with them."

Maralyn agreed, but she collected every egg. This turtle proved to be the most rewarding of all up to that time. In future we would look especially for the female turtles, recognized by their short tails, because we found, in addition, that their livers were sweeter and, for their size, bulkier than the male's liver. The male turtles with their long, grotesque tails were generally larger and in plan, of a more oval shape. Apart from the extra meat, the male had little more to offer than the additional roes from above the pelvic bone.

115

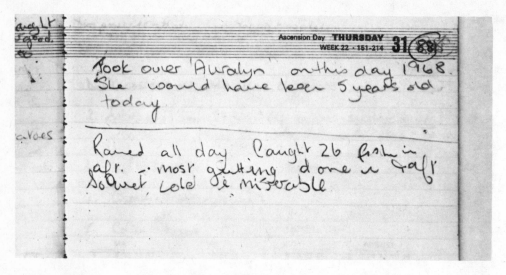

Took over 'Auralyn' on this day 1968. She would have been 5 years old today.

Rained all day. Caught 26 fish in aft. - most getting done u raft. So wet, cold & miserable

Shark attacks   Maralyn finished the work and came into the raft out of the sun. I had no appetite but Maralyn encouraged me with small pieces of the choicest meat. Every time I woke from a doze during the day she would pass pieces of meat to me. Reluctantly I would take a piece and slowly eat.

It was later that day that we were first buffeted by sharks. Swimming fast close to the surface the sharks would repeatedly strike the underside of the raft. Time and again the sharks would collide with our rumps with bruising force, making us cry out with pain. There was little flesh on our bones to absorb the blows, and there was no warning of an onslaught. The pain was acute when a blow struck the base of our spines or a sore place. We could think of nothing that would drive the creatures away.

Maralyn wondered if they were after us. I doubted this but I was very curious as to why we should be subjected to their sadistic sport. The 'attacks' continued periodically through the night and for many days ahead, although not every day. Our bodies became severely bruised and we dreaded the appearance of the sharks.

116

May 31st
(88)

Maralyn

When fish were plentiful I enjoyed fishing although the added work made me tired, especially on the several occasions when I had to kill and butcher a turtle.

May 31st was a wet, cold day made even more miserable by the fact that *Auralyn* would have been five years old on this day. How much we had done in five years! It was hard to believe that part of our life was over, and somehow and somewhere we must start all over again.

Day after day it rained and gradually the wind and seas increased. Rain drove at us horizontally and the inside of the raft became water-logged. Constantly, we had to bale to keep down the water level. We dipped sponges into the water and squeezed them into our biscuit tin which was then emptied over the side. Gallons and gallons of water descended on us and, after replacing all the bad water in our containers, we had to throw the rest of the water overboard.

Maurice

June 1st
(89)

We hung some of the fish fillets from the morning catch along the stays of our dinghy mast to dry in the sun. These we hoped would keep if fish later became scarce, although we knew that vital vitamins would have been destroyed.

We rested during the afternoon in the raft away from the tormenting sun. The clear, bright sky however was quickly replaced by menacing black clouds to the north. I checked the wind; it was still blowing steadily from the south-east. The approaching dark clouds could not be for us, I thought. But I was wrong. The sun slowly became obscured and a chilliness came over us.

Very quickly the wind stopped and when it came again, it blew from the north, lightly at first. We struggled into our oilskin jackets, knowing that this wind would bring the rain. Maralyn arranged the bucket beneath our water catchment and covered our books with a sail bag. I fastened down the

117

"The clear, bright sky however was quickly replaced by menacing black clouds to the north."

flap across the entrance and looked as I did so towards the advancing line of cloud. High, grey clouds in advance of the squall grew darker as the angle steepened towards a solid black curtain of rain. The wind grew stronger and with it came the first few drops followed by the increasing sound of the approach of heavy rain beating a massive tattoo on the surface of the sea.

118

Squalls, and rain

We made ourselves as snug as possible. The biscuit tin which we would use for baling and the sponges were placed ready for the downpour. The sky darkened as though the light had finished for the day and then the onslaught began. It seemed as though the clouds would discharge their complete burden on to us personally. The rain drummed with incredible violence on the canopy and flattened the waves.

We began bailing almost immediately, the canopy filtering the rain like a fine spray. We worked hard mopping up water on the side tubes and around ourselves, squeezing the saturated sponges into the biscuit tin. The tin would be full in less than a minute and I would then empty it outside.

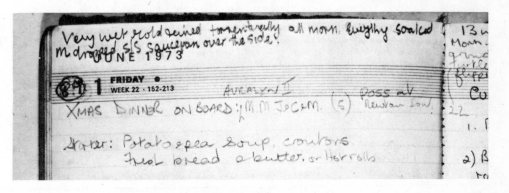

Hour after hour the downpour continued. Maralyn would patiently top up our water containers as the bucket filled. When our containers were full she would then pass the bucket to me and I would empty the water over the side.

Nothing could be seen through the rain and we had to shout to make ourselves heard. It poured with increasing ferocity until after many hours a startling flash of lightning followed by the deep resonant boom of thunder proclaimed a slackening of the rain. As the rain decreased the day grew lighter although solid cloud still covered the sky. I left Maralyn to finish baling the raft while I started on the dinghy.

Our fish, hung up to dry, had been reduced to a soggy mess. I threw it away, and settled down to catch some more for our evening meal.

Rain and cold   When it rained we wore our oilskin jackets but our bodies were always chilled due to being immersed up to the waist in cold water. We were never dry. Everything we touched was wet and would remain so; our few clothes, our books and the sextant.

With the flooding of the dinghy the water washed dried blood and turtle excreta from hidden corners of the boat and it contaminated our water in the plastic containers because of ill-fitting caps. So this water always needed replacing and it had to be collected in the bucket and painstakingly transferred to the containers a cupful at a time.

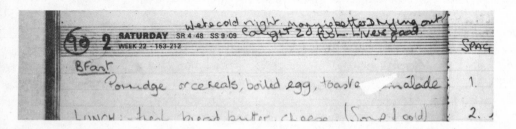

June 2nd   We now had rain almost every day. How we longed to see
(90)   the bright sky again. Never, we told ourselves, would we again complain about the heat of the sun. Conditions were very miserable and we found it impossible to rest. The sky was always overcast and squalls would follow one another across the sky. When one squall passed us by, it would appear to turn and approach us from another direction. The wind and sea tossed the raft and dinghy about like corks. There was no escape. Once started the rainstorms would last several hours and towards the end we would slump in exhaustion unable to bale any more. Between the rain we were able to fish and prepare our meal, but before we could eat the rain would invariably re-start.

It was impossible for us to sit outside in the rain because of the cold. We found what shelter we could under the raft's canopy, the entrance of which had to be firmly closed.

Unfortunately, after several weeks of use the *Velcro* material used for securing the entrance grew tired and would

120

We were wet, cold and ill not stay shut in anything above a light wind. Then I had to sit for most of the day and night holding the cover shut with my hands. Sleep came only during brief respites from the squalls and rainstorms.

To make matters worse I developed a fever during this time and became plagued with diarrhoea. This meant frequent visits to the dinghy to make use of the 'outside loo'. We had adopted the empty biscuit tin for the calls of nature and, in our weakened state, we found it uncomfortable and painful to crouch over this small tin.

We were now existing at a primeval level where the layers of civilization had been stripped away from us. We found our bodily functions unembarrassing and it was surprisingly easy to stay clean. We would wash in sea water, clean our teeth and comb our hair, and in my case, my beard. It was usually far too cold to sit out in the rain and we did not often take advantage of the frequent downpours for bathing.

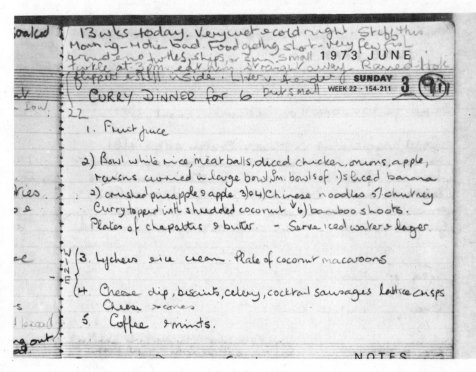

13 wks today. Very wet & cold night. Stiff this Morning – Note bad. Food getting short – very few fish grinding no turtles, ships, or sun. Small **1973 JUNE** Turtle at 3pm. eat him strongly away. Raised tail flipper & still inside. Liver v. tender! **SUNDAY** **WEEK 22 · 154-211** **3**

CURRY DINNER for 6 Ducks small 22

1. Fruit juice

2) Bowl white rice, meat balls, diced chicken, onions, apple, raisins curried in large bowl. Sm. bowls of :) sliced banana

2) crushed pineapple & apple 3)&4) Chinese noodles 5) chutney Curry topped with shredded coconut ✓6) bamboo shoots. Plates of chapattis & butter. – Serve iced water & lager.

3. Lychees & ice cream. Plate of coconut macaroons

4. Cheese dip, biscuits, celery, cocktail sausages lattice crisps Cheese > cones

5. Coffee & mints.

NOTES

Maralyn

June 3rd
(91) Food became very scarce as our drift was too fast and the fish disappeared in bad weather. To control our drift Maurice had streamed my oilskin trousers in a bight of rope. This drogue kept the back of the raft facing the waves but, occasionally, it would get tangled with the dinghy warp and, as it lost its effectiveness, the raft would slew round and face the oncoming waves. It became a frantic struggle to free the drogue before the raft was pooped. Often we didn't succeed in time and a deluge of sea water would fill the raft.

Most of the time in the raft we didn't wear any clothes. What we had left was just one shirt each, one pair of shorts each, one sweater and two pairs of my underpants all of which we stored in a canvas kit-bag. We wore shirts if we went outside in order to protect our bodies from sunburn but these became impregnated with salt and chafed our bodies. We were more comfortable without them. To try and keep warm when it rained we both wore our oilskin jackets, but continual immersion in sea water made them chafe the skin, especially on our wrists and arms.

June 5th, my diary recorded as being our worst day. We had to bale throughout the night and had never been so cold since leaving England.

Maurice

The wind had increased from the south during the night bringing big seas which broke with great menace around us. The waves became so large that we doubted the raft's ability to withstand their assault. We appeared to be drifting too fast; the trousers were not working well as a drogue but I could not think of anything else that would help to slow us down. We were reluctant to risk tying any more valuable equipment to our slender drogue line.

June 5th
(93) Daylight the next morning revealed a wild scene. Heavy cloud covered the sky and the spray from the grey, breaking

122

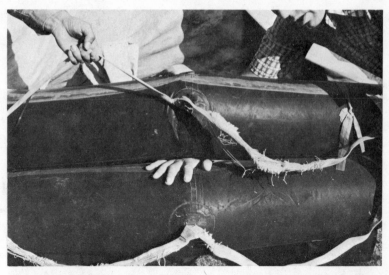

Safely ashore, Maurice puts his hand in between the inflated tubes of the raft showing where the splits occurred which threatened to swamp it when we were in the Pacific. At that time the lower tube was also deflated owing to punctures. Note the fraying of the life-lines.

The great storm waves continually soaked us. The raft and dinghy gyrated up the steep walls of the waves and were flung violently against each other. Frequently, the warps had to be freed from the underside of the raft. It seemed to our exhausted minds as though we had always had weather like this.

"I will try and fish," I said balefully after several hours of watching the waves and deciding, inevitably, that our hunger must be satisfied soon and that the seas would not subside.

Maralyn watched my perilous transfer from the raft to the dinghy. "Do be careful," she said, I shouted to reassure her and started to bale out the dinghy with the biscuit tin. Waves would send splashes of water into the nearly empty dinghy frustrating my attempts to drain it completely. The movement was very violent and sitting on the thwart became a trial. The friction between the rubber seat, the salt water and my skin aggravated my sores and any movement became agonizing.

I cut up pieces of fish, baited the hook and trailed it in the water. Few fish were to be seen, they had all disappeared. Only

123

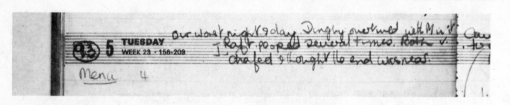

Our worst night and day

an occasional straggler swam past out of the hundreds that were with us the previous day. No fish seemed to be interested.

The dinghy would collide with the raft, knocking me off my precarious seat and then the two craft would drift quickly apart until the warps pulled up tight with a jerk that would again dislodge me off the thwart. The position was impossible and I told Maralyn so.

"Come into the raft then," she said. "It looks too dangerous out there."

"If we can't keep replacing this bait we shall have to wait until we find another turtle," I shouted over the wind. "I'll clear up and come in."

This decision came one minute too late. I gazed with horror behind the raft to where an enormous wall of water was building up. The raft was bound to be engulfed. Maralyn could not see the wave and I shouted a warning. In that fractional span of time I could not estimate the height of the wave but I remember being appalled by its size.

Amazingly the raft rode up the side of the wave; it had escaped. The dinghy, however, seemed to be out of phase and I lay low in the boat gripping the life-lines tightly. The wave broke, pouring its solid mass over the little craft. A chilling blackness covered me, the weight of water pressing me hard to the floor. The world turned dizzily and I found myself sinking to, what I imagined was a great depth. As I swam desperately to gain the surface the discovery of the dinghy upturned above me sent me, for an instant, into a panic.

I broke surface alongside the dinghy, my eyes searched my near surroundings and I saw Maralyn's face peering anxiously from the raft.

124

"In that fractional span of time I could not estimate the height of the wave, but I remember being appalled by its size."

Maralyn

June 5th
(93) I had felt myself going up as if in a lift and realized I was on the crest of a huge wave. I gazed at the dinghy below me and suddenly the raft began charging down the face of the wave towards it. I expected them to crash together and braced myself for the impact but before I reached it the dinghy was flying in the air and disappeared in a smother of foam.

Unable to speak or do anything, I gazed at the upturned dinghy. I can hardly describe my relief when I saw Maurice's head break the surface behind the dinghy. It took many minutes of combined effort before he was 'landed' in the raft. As he rested I turned my attention to the dinghy and watched a plastic container go scudding by, just out of reach.

The oars, water carriers and compass were tied to the dinghy so before we could right it we had to fumble to undo the fastenings and bring as much as we could into the raft. Then began the herculean task of turning the dinghy over. Several times we almost succeeded when the wind caught it and pulled it away from our grasp and it flopped once more face down on the sea. Finally, we managed to right it and lash everything back in place. We were both exhausted by our efforts and, as we lay resting, we took stock of our position. Our bait had disappeared and also all our fishing gear.

Maurice

That night it was impossible to sleep; waves buffeted the raft and constantly moved our equipment from its various stowed positions. We spent much of our time restowing everything. Occasionally, a wave would strike us hard and water would splash up the canopy and cascade into the raft. Then we would have to bale furiously. This always dismayed us because salt water on the canopy meant that we needed much rain in the future to clean the salt away before it could be used for drinking. Rarely did we manage to get the water below the level of our hips. Our legs, thighs and buttocks were

126

being continually chafed on the black rubber adding to our
discomfort. Because of the deep, ulcer-like sores on my rump
and hips and it was impossible to find a comfortable position
for my body.

Suddenly, as though we had been struck by some giant's
hammer, we found ourselves climbing violently towards the
vertical propelled by a blow from a wave that broke right over
us. The entrance flap burst open and a mass of water
exploded into the raft. After the torrent of water had stopped
and we had realized that the raft was still upright we began
the tormenting task of emptying the raft once more.

Maralyn and I looked towards each other in the blackness
of the night as we sat back, tired out with our efforts.

"What will happen if the raft capsizes?" Maralyn asked. I
was angry at this question because I did not know the answer.
Surely she can work it out for herself, I thought, but, perhaps,
it is just reassurance she needs.

I said, "I don't think it will capsize, but we must prepare
ourselves for that to happen. Get what is left of the tinned
food, the knives and tin opener and put them all into the
haversack."

We groped in the darkness and placed everything we could
find inside the haversack we had used for our emergency
pack. Then Maralyn found a piece of cord and lashed it to
the raft.

"If the raft goes over at least we shall be able to save those
few things," I said. "It will be very difficult to right it in these
seas."

"I don't feel like dying, not tonight anyway," Maralyn said,
feeling for my hand. It was then, I think, that I fully
appreciated the extent of Maralyn's tenacity for life; it would
not be any failing on her part if we did not survive.

The storm lasted for four days during which time we
caught no fish and we had to use our precious supply of canned
food. Fresh bait would now be essential before we could start
fishing again.

127

Petrel. This is the most familiar of oceanic birds. It is the size of a swallow and flies close to the water with erratic wing beats, and snatches its food from the sea without alighting. However, it occasionally pats the water with its feet giving the impression of walking. Not a strong swimmer. Spends most of its time at sea except during the breeding periods.

Maralyn

"Do we have any more pins?" asked Maurice. "I think so," I cautiously replied. "I'll have a look." I tipped out the contents of a small polythene box and found three pins, two large and one small.

Maurice reminded me that the large ones were not as useful as the small ones as the hook was too large for the smaller fish we usually caught. Later that day I began to bend the pins into hooks. I tried to bend a large pin but to my horror it snapped in half. Gingerly I bent the small one and made a reasonable hook. I found a length of string and doubled it through the spring loop—we could not afford to lose this one. All we had to get now was bait and we were back in the fishing business.

9 We Belonged to the Sea

Maralyn

June 6th (94) Fortune smiled on us next day; the gale had subsided and some hefty bumps underneath us denoted a turtle. I leaned out of the vent hole and waited for the animal to surface. When it did I grabbed a flipper and held on tightly; usually at this stage it didn't struggle very much and we found this was the best routine to adopt. Meanwhile, Maurice got into the dinghy and hauled himself alongside to reach over and take hold of the turtle. As soon as he had a firm grip on it I let go and wriggled back into the raft down the vent chute. I then got into the dinghy and together we heaved the turtle over the side and with a great effort turned it upside down. This procedure was always accompanied with great flapping and clapping of flippers and we usually had several battle scars after the fight. Twice Maurice sustained very nasty bites on his ankle and once as I sat on the thwart getting my breath back I received a hefty nip on my bottom: fortunately the only damage was to my dignity!

Twenty-fourth turtle We hauled the huge female turtle into the aft section of the dinghy. She was large and we reasoned she could be full of eggs. We decided to keep her until the next day and returned to the raft to drool over the thought of eggs for breakfast. That evening we opened a small, rusty tin of sardines—of all the tinned food on board the yacht I had to bring tinned fish!

Next morning we went out to the dinghy to kill the turtle. While we were deciding who should do what, along came a male turtle.

Twenty-fifth turtle Maurice leaned over the side and got a firm grip on the turtle's front flippers. It lay partially submerged in the water

June 7th
(95) without struggling while I cleared out the forward section of the dinghy. In the meantime Maurice had caught hold of one of the turtle's rear flippers and as soon as I was ready, he transferred the rear flipper to my hand. Still the creature did not struggle.

Hampered by the presence of the female turtle underfoot which at that moment had burst into frantic activity it was difficult for me to pull effectively and I left most of the work to Maurice. The friction of the shell on the fabric made our task more difficult, although throughout the operation this turtle did not struggle. Eventually the unfortunate creature was upside down in the front of the dinghy. Now, we had a choice; which one to keep and which one to kill! From previous experience we found that males often gave up and died before the females, so we decided to kill and eat the newly captured male. As we began to collect the steaks the rain started once more. We took half the meat and liver inside the raft and hoped the rest would stay fresh until the following day.

June 8th
(96) Next morning to our surprise the turtle meat was still fresh and we were also pleased to see a small shoal of trigger fish nearby. Using some of the meat I tried fishing but immediately realized these fish were too wary. It was obviously a new shoal, unused to the hook and very suspicious of the dangling pieces of turtle meat. I fed them intestines and some meat—just to encourage them.

By now they had got over their initial shyness and fifteen trigger fish and one tender milk-fish tumbled into the dinghy in rapid succession. Our female turtle was still alive and we decided to keep her to celebrate the following Sunday, exactly fourteen weeks since *Auralyn* was sunk.

I found it helped morale to have a day to look forward to and any event was made a celebration day. For example April 20th, Good Friday, April 22nd Easter Monday, April 23rd St. George's Day, April 24th my birthday and April 29th my uncle's birthday. This way we always managed to be looking forward and not brooding over the past.

130

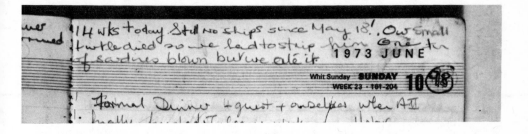

14 wks today. Still no ships since May 18'. Our small turtle died so we had to strip him. One tin of sardines blown but we ate it 1973 JUNE

Whit Sunday SUNDAY 10
WEEK 23 · 161–204

Formal Dinner + guest + ourselves when AI

Maurice

June 10th
(98)

Single booby birds would settle during the late afternoon on our dinghy and digest their latest catch of fish. Their digestive processes invariably meant a large evacuation and within a short space of time the dinghy and all our water containers would be covered white. This upset us especially when we considered how it might contaminate our drinking water.

When a large blue-faced booby landed one day on the raft we became annoyed at the mess it was making. I hauled the dinghy in close; the bird showed no fear and continued to preen itself. Even then, with the booby in grasping distance, we did not think of it as food. There was no real need as we had ample fish.

I lifted one of the paddles and struck the booby a blow, not to injure it but to make it fly away. With a squawk and an almost surprised look in its eyes it flopped into the water between the raft and the dinghy. It did not fly away but started to regurgitate four whole flying fish in front of us. A fine supplement to our supper, we thought, as we scooped them out of the water.

Maralyn

During the night we caught a small turtle and were very frustrated to find in the morning that it had died! It was our celebration day and we wanted our female and the eggs but

131

June 11/12th
(99/100)
instead we had to eat the small turtle. We decided on another celebration day, Tuesday June 12th, we would then have been one hundred days in the raft.

We decided we needed a change of diet and as the sea was calmer we began fishing again. The fish were not very enthusiastic and when a large sea bird landed on top of the raft we discussed the possibilities of catching him. Boobies had always been flying around us and often would land on dinghy or raft while we were fishing. Usually we drove them off by giving them a swipe with a paddle, they would flop into the sea with a disconcerted squawk, looking completely perplexed. Often the bird would fly back on to the raft and only after a further swipe would the idea that it wasn't welcome sink in.

This time we tolerated the mess and tried our utmost to make it feel welcome; no wonder it looked so puzzled! Oblivious of his impending doom the bird sat serenely on the overhead tube digesting its meal.

Wrapping part of the towel round my hand I stretched up and caught its foot. As I dragged it into the raft Maurice wrapped the other towel round its beak. Muffled squawks came from inside the towel and as we unwrapped it, the bird lunged forward and caught my thumb in its beak.

Any pity I had for it disappeared. I wrung its neck quickly and then sat back nursing my injured thumb. The gash was small but very deep and took a long time to heal. We plucked the bird in the dinghy taking care to make sure that the raft was to windward. Feathers littered the sea and hordes of trigger fish gathered round and nibbled at them.

The trigger fish showing their usual greediness grabbed at everything in sight. I twisted off one of the bird's wings and held the slightly bloody end over the side. The fish held on to the shreds of meat and I flipped them into the dinghy before they realized what was happening. I caught several by this method and, of course, it saved the precious hook. The bird's flesh was dark red and very sweet, but such a change from fish or turtle that we thoroughly enjoyed it.

Imagine our chagrin when in the morning we found our

132

The Booby

Booby. They lead oceanic lives only returning to land for the breeding season. We saw both red-footed and blue-footed varieties. They are so named because of their looks and action. They are completely unafraid of humans. Main food is flying fish.

June 12th
(100)

female turtle dead. It saved us the struggle of killing it but defeated our blood catching operation as we now had a real liking for the congealed fluid. It was sweet and tasted very much like liver and there was plenty of it. We had looked forward so much to this turtle yet already she had disappointed us. When we opened her up we were further disillusioned as she had no eggs and very little fatty substance, although the steaks, as usual, were very tender.

We have since discovered that several species of these cold blooded creatures are almost identical in appearance. The turtles with yellow-green fat were without doubt green turtles, but Ridley turtles are very similar and the only way of identifying them is through the patterns on the head. We caught several turtles which had a pronounced hump. We didn't attach any significance to it but this shape usually

133

Loggerhead Turtle. This variety has no green fatty substance and the back has a pronounced hump. The meat is equally as tender as that of the Green Turtle.

means it is a logger-head turtle. Although only the green turtle is revered for its flesh we found each turtle extremely tender and could not detect any difference. The taste we found was a cross between veal and chicken with a dash of crab meat, if anyone can imagine such a combination!

Maurice

Our part of the ocean was now proving to be extremely bountiful and we never ceased to be fascinated and amazed at the abundance of life. A multitude of fish swam below us in gaudy layers; spine-foots, trigger fish, milk-fish and wolf herrings abounded. Our periods of regular fishing would

Wolf Herring (Dorab). They seemed to be about two feet long but they always swam deep below us. Brilliant blue with vivid yellow tails.

134

Jacks and
young shark

Jack. A marine fish of wide distribution. A golden colour all over. Size approximately nine inches long. It had a prominent ridge each side near the tail.

break the monotony of the day. We would fish morning and afternoon and invariably our most prolific fish was the trigger fish. Indeed so anxious were these fish to be caught that sometimes we could bring two or three out on the same piece of bait.

Some days we would catch over one hundred trigger fish. On other days we would catch a dozen or less and on odd days none at all. We have calculated that our average daily catch must have been approximately forty fish and if we caught fish on one hundred days this would make a total of four thousand fish, or more. The catching was the easiest part, the gutting and cutting up was time consuming and exhausting. The softened flesh on our fingers had been chafed to the bone by the continual use of the scissors.

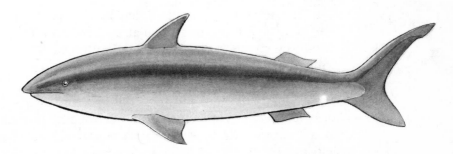

Young Shark. Approximately three feet long. The skin appeared to be brownish-grey when in the water and became silver-grey when taken out.

135

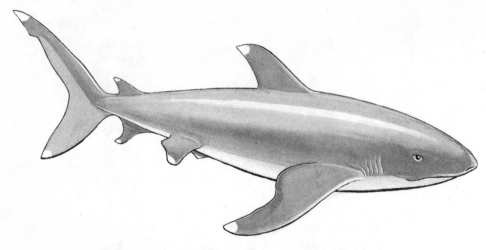

White-tipped Shark. Approximately ten to twelve feet long. Silver-grey with white tips to the fins and tail. This is the variety which continually bumped the bottom of the raft.

Sharks   Unfortunately, their eagerness to grab the bait had other detracting features. We would wash our hands over the side and have them seized by the trigger fish, their small mouths biting into our flesh. Sometimes they broke the skin before we could withdraw our hands. At one time we even considered the plan that if we lost all our hooks or required fresh bait we could use our fingers as bait. For their size we considered the trigger fish more fierce and more aggressive than the much feared sharks.

In fact, although we realized that sharks have the power to kill men, we did not find them at all ferocious. They would swim contentedly amongst the shoal of fish we had attracted without disturbing our fishing. Care had to be taken to ensure the sharks did not take the bait otherwise we would soon lose a precious hook and, possibly, the line. In tropical waters their food is so abundant that they showed no interest in us at all nor in any of the turtles' blood and carcasses we jettisoned. Apart from their peculiar desire to buffet our black raft we had no fear of them; we came to accept them almost as companionable creatures. I really think they are cowards

136

because they would hasten away whenever we splashed the water above them.

Huge white-tipped sharks and much smaller varieties would cruise around us escorted often by gaudy pilot fish. A single whale shark, the largest fish in the world and an extremely rare sighting, we saw below us one day. Its slow, lethargic movement, its broad spotted body and blunt nose made it easily distinguishable from other sharks.

Maralyn

When we first butchered a turtle during our misadventure I kept a wary lookout for sharks because of the prodigious amount of blood. Blood will send sharks into a frenzy, I had been told. Not once did sharks come close during the killing of fish, turtle or birds. Occasionally an odd one was glimpsed cruising around but they usually kept their distance. It was only when they were in large groups that they made themselves offensive; the gang syndrome.

Many dorado swam below us, their vivid luminous blue-green shapes sparkling in the clear blue water. Not once were these alluring fish attracted to our hooks. We watched them as they cruised slowly to and fro, as though on patrol. Sometimes, we saw them make great bursts of speed and once or twice we were fascinated to see them jump well clear of the water after flying fish.

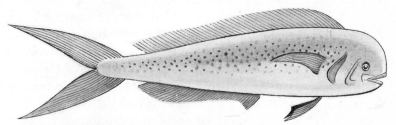

Dolphin Fish (Dorado). A brilliant blue/green body. The male's forehead becomes more domed with age. Can reach speeds of thirty-five miles per hour chasing flying fish and can leap out of the water to a height of eighteen feet. Size approximately four feet long.

137

Frigate Bird. It is recorded as having forty per cent more wing area than other sea birds of similar bulk. It has vast reserves of power and can soar and glide effortlessly. It is known to have flown at a height of 4,000 feet. The plumage is not fully waterproof and therefore they rarely settle on water. They do not have webbed feet. The male (upper drawing) has a bright red throat pouch which it can inflate.

Maurice

Boobies and frigate birds

We had many visits from green, loggerhead and Ridley turtles, distinguished often only by their shell patterns. We often found sucker fish (*remora remora*), always in pairs, attached to the plastron shells of the turtles.

The days were rare when we did not see a booby bird and, probably, we might encounter two or three species on one day. There were the blue-faced or masked boobies and brown boobies. They are goose-sized birds with heavy streamlined bodies and are of the same family as the northern gannet.

A booby would soar over the sea waiting for flying fish to break cover. It would then plunge into the waves, re-appearing in a moment juggling with a fish in its beak. After swallowing the catch, it would then take up its vigil once more. Although we would invariably remove whole flying fish from their gullets when we killed them, boobies would also feed on the shoals of trigger fish around us.

We would frequently sit fascinated watching frigate birds soaring motionless high above us and watching them chase booby birds, pecking at them until the unfortunate boobies disgorged their fish to escape from their tormentors. The frigate birds would swoop down and pick up the fish in mid-air. This piracy, we felt sure, was not their only means of livelihood.

Dolphins and other large fish would chase shoals of flying fish and the frigate birds would snatch them when they leapt clear of the water. The latter also appeared to pick up anything that floated on the surface; they were attracted to pieces of surplus turtle fat we had discarded.

Despite their partly webbed feet we never saw frigate birds enter the water. I learned later that their feathers would soon become water-logged and they would find difficulty in taking off from the sea. Their long wing span supports a relatively small black coloured body. We were able to distinguish between the sexes, the male having a distinctive red throat. It surprised us to see them so far from land.

Petrels, truly birds of the sea, came in varying numbers. Although we found them no larger than seven inches in length, they are apparently related to the albatross and shearwater. They flew close to the water with erratic wingbeats, sometimes singly, often in small dispersed flocks. The storm petrels were often attracted to us by the turtle fat we threw over the side, snatching pieces from the sea without alighting.

The petrel's diet is normally drifting plankton. They would hover close to the surface with fluttering wings with their feet moving in the water as though they were walking. After alighting on the water they found little difficulty in becoming airborne again. The storm petrels that we watched were dark coloured and had square tails and short black legs and feet.

Another bird that sometimes came to us was of a solid grey colour about twelve inches in length. It had webbed feet and we thought that it might have been a noddy of the gull and tern family. We caught one and we found its red meat excellent. Why they should have been so far from land was a mystery to us.

As well as our particular region of plenty, we felt sure that there must also be 'desert' areas in which little or no life existed. Fortune smiled upon us; the currents and winds were to keep us in this prolific zone.

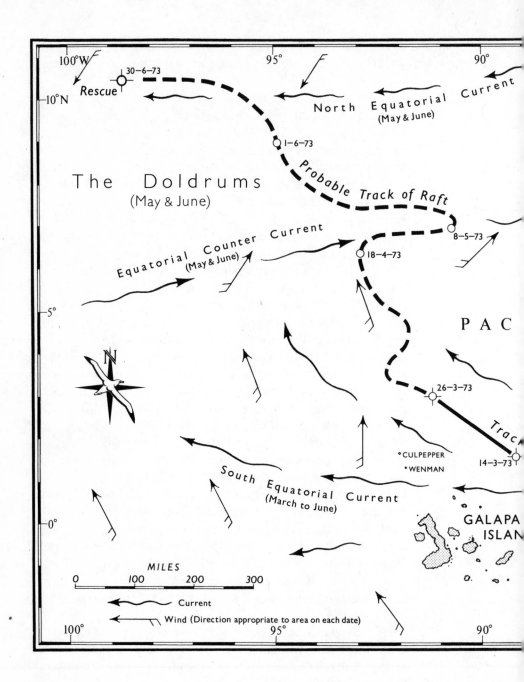

The Doldrums
(May & June)

North Equatorial Current
(May & June)

Probable Track of Raft

Equatorial Counter Current
(May & June)

South Equatorial Current
(March to June)

PAC

Rescue   30-6-73

1-6-73

8-5-73

18-4-73

26-3-73

14-3-73

Trac

CULPEPPER
WENMAN

GALAPA
ISLAN

N

MILES
0   100   200   300

Current
Wind (Direction appropriate to area on each date)

100°W   95°   90°
10°N
5°
0°
100°   95°   90°

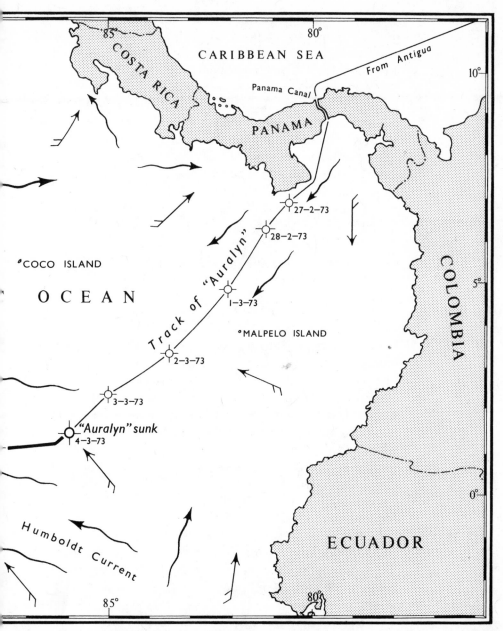

Here is shown the track of the raft together with the prevailing winds and currents experienced during the period of the year that the raft was in the area. The winds are shown by means of feathered arrows. The currents are shown with curly arrows.

June 16th
(104)

The thunderstorms came and went with increasing frequency. Then the wind increased and low, dark clouds scudded quickly across the sky foretelling the coming of another storm. Apprehensively we watched the waves heighten between periods of torrential driving rain. More and more our discomfort grew with the violently increasing motion; rain was now an ever present facet of our daily routine. It was difficult for us to imagine what it had been like to be warm and dry. My salt water sores were becoming daily more unbearable. The pain from these sapped my spirit and I found little contentment in living. I was in a state of abject misery. Rest had been a luxury that we had both forgotten. Now all our efforts went towards survival. There was no prospect of fishing in those conditions and we expended our energy ridding the raft of water. Even when it was not raining waves would send water crashing over us and we would start all over again.

More storms

Each hour went by slowly and with tedious monotony. I wondered just how we could survive the next hour. Yet Maralyn appeared undaunted, she encouraged me to keep baling with promises of good things when the storm subsided. She spoke of the luxury of sitting there eating meat and the greenish fat from the green turtles. We talked while we worked, describing to each other the relative merits of the male and female turtle. We could no longer talk of the food we would eat had we been rescued, the prospects were too slender at that time and it would have depressed us further. These discussions we referred to as 'morale boosters' and our discomfort was tolerable while we dreamed of eating our turtle steaks in warm sunshine.

Reality frequently came upon us as another load of water had to be cleared, or the raft would need inflating again, or the cloths that we had placed in the gaps that had opened up between the tubes would need wringing or replacing. There was no respite.

The storm continued for four more days and we tried to keep warm beneath our oilskin jackets. This was impossible, however, and the jackets chafed our bodies. White blisters

142

Noddy

Noddy. A member of the tern family. Grey, the size of a small pigeon.

appeared on our paunches and arms. We longed to rid ourselves of those jackets, but we feared the cold. Sitting very
cramped in the small space of the raft exercise was difficult
and, in any case, I became reluctant to move for fear of shift-
ing on to an ulcerated spot.

Nothing was new and our whole existence was as though
we belonged to the sea. We could see and feel and hear only
the things directly about us. Our association with the sea was
no longer detached. It appeared as though we knew no other
life. I had stopped dreaming of our life before or after this
misadventure.

Our hunger began to increase our distress. We shared our
meagre storm rations of one tin a day. Ironically, now that
we had ample water our thirst had long since been satisfied.
The perverse malignity of fate now adjudged that we discard
every drop of water we collected.

Another   On the second day of the storm the dinghy became water-
capsize   logged and required emptying urgently. I clambered into the
dinghy to bale it out, after which I would try to fish to satisfy
our hunger. I took with me our last remaining hook. When I
had got the dinghy very nearly clear of water, a wave broke

across it and, taken by surprise, I was flung clear as the boat
capsized. As I surfaced I saw Maralyn at the raft entrance.
"Have you got the hook?" she called out anxiously. I lifted
my left arm and opened my fist. To my surprise and
Maralyn's delight I had gripped our last valuable hook
firmly when I had been tipped out.

I swam to the raft and passed Maralyn the hook and then
clambered aboard. Then began the struggle to right the
dinghy. Once more the combined effect of the wind and the
weight of the immersed water containers defied our efforts
to turn the dinghy over. We struggled time and again to lift
the dinghy and each time the effort sapped at our
depleting strength.

"We'll have to untie them all," Maralyn said. The thought
of untying the knots securing those containers irritated me. I
said, "Let's have one more go." We tried to lift once more
without any success. Vexed, I untied the containers and got
them into the raft. Our next attempt at lifting the dinghy
succeeded. Having replaced all the containers we retreated to
the relative peace of the raft. However, our troubles were not
yet over.

On the last day of the storm the dinghy turned over again,
this time without either of us on board, but righting it was not
difficult and we felt for the first time that the wind was easing
but our compass and one of the oars had broken loose and
disappeared. Although big seas still troubled us we were sure
that the storm had passed.

Maralyn

On the fourth day of the storm we had caught a medium-
sized female turtle and dropped it in the dinghy with a rope
round its rear flipper. We had lost all our bait but this turtle
would provide us with food and the means of obtaining other
food. It was too rough to kill it but we kept a careful eye on it.
The storm was blowing itself out but the final blow was yet to
be dealt to us. Once again our dinghy overturned in a welter
of foam and this time both of us were concerned for our turtle.

144

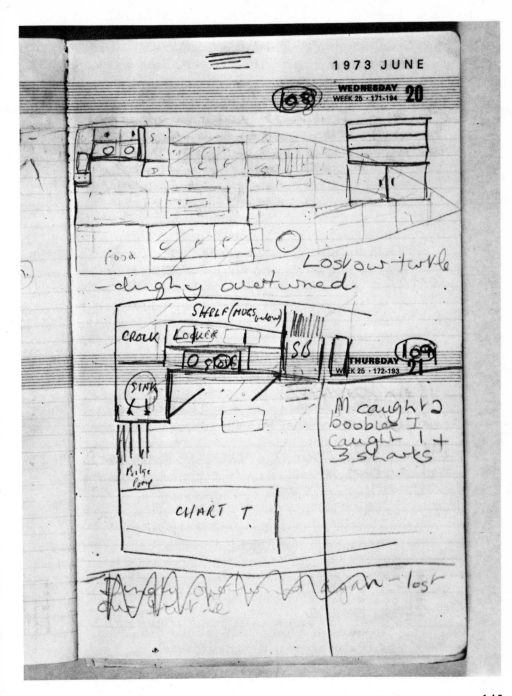

Lost our turtle

—dinghy overturned

SHELF (MUGS, now)

CROCK   LOCKER

O STOVE

SINK

SB

M caught 2
boobies I
caught 1 +
3 sharks

Bilge
Pump

CHART T

dinghy overturned again — lost
our turtle

June 20th (108) Frantically, we hauled the dinghy close and lifted up one end, the turtle was still there! I began to haul it in and realized the rope was slipping. The turtle was almost within grasp and I reached out for it; my hands passed over its shell but it slipped through my fingers and swam away. I was left holding the rope, the remains of two half-hitches looped in the end.

Once more depression settled on us; we were tired, wet, cold, miserable, in fact, no words are adequate to describe our mood. We had lived in anoraks for days and nights on end and the chafing was adding to our discomfort. My legs were now covered with salt water sores and it was difficult to find a comfortable position. But my discomfort was nothing compared to Maurice's. Although his chest pains had eased the sores on his hips and the base of his spine increased in area and were now open, raw wounds. I had some antiseptic cream and large plasters, but this only helped for a short time, then they would come off because of being soaked in sea water. He couldn't see these sores himself and I kept telling him they were only small spots but, in fact, the sore on his spine was at least three-quarters of an inch across and very deep. If only it could have been kept dry it would heal but there was no chance of that.

June 21st (109) The seas were now calmer and the sun occasionally broke through the covering of cloud to dispense its welcome warmth. To pass the time I knelt by the doorway watching the shoals of fish congregate again; we urgently needed bait so that we could start fishing. During the afternoon a school of sharks kept circling around us, sometimes bumping the raft. Maurice sat and dozed next to me. Several times a small shark swam past just below the surface and about a foot away from me. As he went by I poked him and my finger ran down his rough skin. I waited until he came round again and without thinking grabbed his tail. Maurice was rudely awakened from his doze by my excited shouts, for although I had a firm grip on its tail I couldn't do anything else.

Maurice held a towel ready and asked me to flip it towards him. I did so and within minutes the shark was firmly encased in a towel. Maurice held its biting end tightly while I retained

146

We catch some sharks a firm grip on its tail. We were sharing the floor of the raft with a fiercely struggling and voracious shark! To our surprise it soon gave up its struggle for life and after fifteen minutes we carefully unwrapped it and gazed at our catch. It was coloured grey and only about two-and-a-half feet long, but there was a lot of meat on it. Maurice went into the dinghy with the fish and began to gut it. While he worked on I again watched the sharks and when another of similar size went past I couldn't resist the temptation and reached into the water and caught it. Approximately the same size as the other it threshed around splashing water over both of us until Maurice again caught the head. I didn't dare let go of the tail, so I leaned over into the dinghy and held it tightly whilst Maurice hit it repeatedly with his knife. Eventually Maurice drove the knife through its gills and told me to let go. It still twitched and jumped but Maurice could control it.

"I've got another, I've got another," I shouted a little later. Maurice hardly able to believe his eyes repeated the procedure and grabbed this one. With one dead shark in the front of the dinghy, another almost expired shark under his feet and a very much alive one in his hands, Maurice implored me to stop catching them as he had no more hands or feet left! We both burst into gales of merriment at the absurd situation.

I went into the dinghy to help gut our catch, the improving weather and the abundance of food lightening the atmosphere. We were almost gay and discussed the possibility of staying in the dinghy to eat our meal, so much pleasanter than sitting in a drab, soggy raft.

As we threw titbits over the side, one by one the shoal of fish grew larger. After starving for the previous few days the prospect of a good meal was wonderful. I cut the shark meat into small pieces and Maurice prepared for fishing. Before casting the bait a blue-footed booby with a rich brown plumage swooped down and with a great flapping and rustling of wings settled itself on the side of the dinghy only two feet away from Maurice. We looked at each other. "Shall we?" I nodded agreement.

Maurice

Its lack of fear at our nearness spelt its doom. I edged closer to it until it was well within grasping distance and still it did not move. The gannet-like bird looked directly at me through large ringed eyes which gave it a somewhat idiotic appearance. After examining me carefully for some seconds it went on preening itself quite unconcerned.

When I reached out and grabbed its neck it gave a cry and struggled to free itself. Maralyn caught hold of its body while I wrung its neck. Its warm, soft body went limp and in less than a minute it was dead.

We laid it down in the dinghy and turned our attention back to the sharks.

Maralyn

More
boobies

I sat on the dinghy thwart with the bird between my knees ready for plucking when a raucous "Ka-a" made me turn round in time to see a second brown booby settling itself calmly in the same spot on the dinghy as its companion. Quite unconcerned, it began to preen itself.

We were astounded; how could they be so stupid! In reply to Maurice's unasked question I shrugged my shoulders and said, "Try, but if he goes it doesn't matter." Well, he didn't go and in a few minutes we had a second bird—one each now! We were elated, our feast was growing to mammoth proportions!

Shark meat wasn't very palatable, and now we didn't have to eat it, only the liver and sweetmeats which we enjoyed. We both continued gutting the sharks and plucking our birds when we noticed a large white booby diving for food. It circled round and round and when he sighted a particularly luscious fish it would fold back its wings and dive into the sea with a loud splash. The momentum must have carried him a long way down as it was many seconds before the bird reappeared, a fish firmly grasped in its beak.

Catching
bobbies

The Booby is of the same family as the gannet.

To enable the bird to eat his catch he had to turn it round and swallow it head first. To accomplish this the booby tossed the fish quickly into the air, caught its head and swallowed. After such a splendid high dive usually resulting in a catch we were amazed how clumsy the bird was when it came to eating. Often we would see it toss the fish into the air, snap its beak and miss! What a waste of energy!

This white booby dived repeatedly each time closer to our dinghy, it was obviously watching the shoal round us. After one particularly close dive it surfaced alongside and as it spread its wings and shook away the drops of water Maurice shouted, "Grab him!" I reacted without thinking and grabbed one of the outstretched wings. I don't know who was the most surprised, the bird or me! Unfortunately, the bird recovered first and gave me a vicious bite on my hand. Cursing, I swung him towards Maurice to let him deal with the bird while I nursed my bleeding hand.

Three birds and three sharks, what a boost for our morale! We kept the shark meat for bait and that evening dined royally on sharks' livers and one-and-a-half birds each!

149

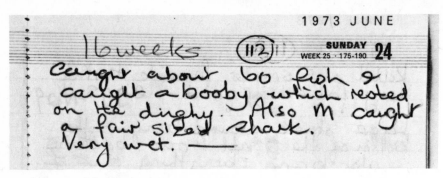

Caught about 60 fish & caught a booby which rested on the dinghy. Also M caught a fair sized shark. Very wet. ———

Maurice

June 24th
(112)

I often sat in the dinghy because there I found great relief from the agony of my sores. Sometimes I would kneel for as long as two hours at a time. During this time I fished while Maralyn mopped the raft dry. One day we basked in a warm sun, which was only momentarily obscured by some low cloud, but we could see dark curtains of rain gradually closing in around us.

"There are quite a few baby sharks around you," Maralyn said.

"Yes, I have to be careful they don't take the bait, otherwise we shall lose the hook," I replied.

This morning I found fishing very uncomfortable, having to sit upright to keep my sores off the abrasive fabric of the dinghy. This spoilt my line of sight and I was only able to dip the bait in the water for a second to avoid the sharks. Nevertheless I had a mounting pile of trigger fish at my feet.

"Why not catch a shark," suggested Maralyn, who was now resting in the raft entrance.

"All right," I said, placing the hook and line carefully to one side: "Anything for a change."

Although I could see the sharks most of the time, they soon became lost to my view as they swam towards the dinghy and disappeared beneath me. I was too stiff and sore to move rapidly from one side of the dinghy to the other, so I leaned across the thwart and called to Maralyn.

"Give me a commentary on the movements of a likely shark."

150

Maurice
catches a
shark

As they circled round I picked out a couple similar in size to the previous ones I had caught and this time Maurice said he would have a go. Being so stiff and sore Maurice could only lean over the side of the dinghy and wait for one to swim by. "Small one just disappeared behind the raft—here he is again—now he's under the dinghy—coming up your side—no, he's off the stern—wait, he's turning round and coming back your side—there he is, grab him!"

Maurice leaned over and grabbed. Unfortunately, he grabbed the wrong one, and the threshing monster was half as big again as the ones I had caught. This one was at least four feet long and it took Maurice all his time to hold it. I got the towel ready and when Maurice flipped its head into the bottom of the dinghy I quickly threw the towel over it.

Using his hands and both feet Maurice held it and transferred the tail into my hands while he reached for the knife. Its blood ran freely and covered our hands and feet yet still it thrashed and jumped. Blood was everywhere and when it was finally dead and lay still we vowed not to catch any more unless they were really 'baby' ones, it was too exhausting.

The shark skin was pearl grey and a very fine texture. It was so beautiful that I wanted to keep it and while Maurice fished I laboriously scraped every bit of flesh away from the skin, intending later to make a purse or some other small object. I rolled it up and stuffed it in a corner of the dinghy, but next day it was dry, crackly, dull and uninteresting so I discarded it.

Larger sharks, which had previously been no trouble, buffeted the bottom of the raft. As the raft deflated our bodies made large protrusions in the floor and were, no doubt, admirable targets. The sharks would approach at high speed but unseen and would hit the raft with a mighty thwack! Often they hit our bodies and jarred our spines until our bones were bruised and tender. Maurice suffered more in these attacks as they hit his open sores and would start them bleeding again. The bangs became agonizing and we dreaded

Shark attacks these times. An attack would last up to half an hour before they went away. We could never decide if they were really being vicious or merely playing, but one fact is certain, their aim was good. Nine times out of ten they would hit us! One strange thing we noticed was the way they always buffeted the raft but not the dinghy, even when we were sitting in the dinghy. I wondered if the colour affected them at all, one craft being black and the other grey.

152

10 Life and Death in the Doldrums

Maralyn

The end of
June Although it was still very wet, the weather had improved, the wind eased and calm days followed. We began to spend as little time as possible in the raft because we found the dampness depressing and uncomfortable. Maurice, unable to sit for long found relief by kneeling in the dinghy for several hours at a time, thereby taking the pressure off his sores.

From dawn until mid morning we stayed in the dinghy fishing, eating and enjoying our outdoor 'picnics'. We still wore our anoraks although by this time our wrists were chafed raw, but it was too cold at night and during the rain showers to be without cover of some sort.

We now spent a long time discussing the places we would visit on our next voyage. Maurice quietly stated he would like to go to Patagonia next time. I knew this was a long-cherished dream of his. "But it's cold down there," I complained.

"Not in summer," retorted Maurice, and began a lengthy lecture on Patagonia, trying to explain why the lonely, windy and wild place held such a fascination for him. His enthusiasm was contagious and soon I was equally enthralled about the country. We talked of hunting and fishing trips, the clothes we would wear and the problem of securing the boat in such open anchorages, it became so vivid in our imagination.

Turtles were very prolific and we now had to chase some away. This amazed us as we didn't expect to find turtles so far from land and especially when some of the females had half-developed eggs inside them.

Many times a large turtle would be accompanied by a small

153

one and once I saw a small one trying to climb on to the back of his protector. We wondered if the young ones latched on to an experienced adult to learn 'sea lore', but this theory lost some of its strength when one morning towards the end of June I caught a very lonesome young turtle.

Turtles usually approached us from behind; often, I believed, being curious about our drogue. Occasionally they would become entangled in the ropes securing the drogue and the pulling and splashing would attract our attention to them, but at other times it was the loud sigh as they exhaled air, or, strangely enough, their pungent odour which announced their presence.

I heard frenzied splashing and gasping behind the raft and undoing the vent popped my head out to see what was going on. "It's a little turtle," I cried, and as Maurice began to move to follow our usual procedure for turtle-catching, I told him to stay where he was. I reached out and disentangled the reptile and hauled him through the vent and deposited him on the floor by Maurice's knees. It was no more than seven inches long with a vividly patterned carapace of pale and dark brown, and the plastron was also patterned with large spots. A row of fierce spikes ran the length of his back. We had noticed these spikes before on young turtles but they blunted and wore flat in the adult ones. Our little 'pet' explored the raft, finally settling down inside a plastic bowl.

Young Turtles. The small turtles which we saw were brilliantly marked and had prominent sharp spines in a ridge down their backs. These wore down as they matured.

154

Next morning we took our turtle out to the dinghy and let
him swim around inside while we fished. Jokingly, I said we
wanted another one to make up a pair and during the
morning I saw another small turtle approaching the raft. I
dived back into the raft and caught the turtle through the
vent and, like the previous one, pulled it into the raft and
emerged triumphant in the doorway dangling it by its flipper.

We let them both run round the dinghy as we compared
them. Our latest arrival was slightly smaller with different
markings and was predominantly brown. They walked over
our feet while we fished and seemed very unconcerned about
the whole thing. That evening we decided to leave them in the
dinghy, and Maurice secured their rear flippers by a short
lashing to the dinghy.

During the first two months we had tried to eke out the very
small supply of food that we had taken from the yacht. We
had finished the treacle and the condensed milk by taking a
spoonful each day. The part-used packet of dates was also

"I heard frenzied splashing and gasping behind the raft and, undoing the vent,
popped my head out to see what was going on."

rationed to one each every other day. Our small bottle of vitamin tablets from the emergency pack becoming 'smarties' and every other day was a 'smartie' day for us. When we had finished these the fish eyes became our 'smarties'.

It seemed a strange thing but we found we needed salt and often we would sit licking our salt-coated fingers. Several times we had our turtle meat soaked in a rain shower and found the meat was insipid. Then we would wash it again in sea water to give it some flavour. The same thing happened with fish livers and fillets. Although, occasionally, we poured some rainwater into the bowl of fillets and left it for about one hour. This seemed to have the effect of marinating the flesh until it became translucent and had a 'cooked' appearance making them tender and not so chewy.

As hook after hook snapped or was taken by larger fish, we had to seek another means of catching them. When gutting fish we dropped entrails and other unwanted pieces into a bucket to avoid fouling the dinghy floor. The bucket would then be emptied over the side and rinsed many times. The trigger fish would tumble over themselves to get at these titbits and on several occasions Maurice scooped a fish out with the bucket.

This gave me an idea. I took the one-gallon container which had held the kerosene. It was made of blue plastic, measured 8″ by 8″ by 7″ wide, and had a carrying handle on the top, the spout being beyond one end of this. I got Maurice to cut a square hole in the side opposite the spout. I now removed the cap from the spout and threaded a baited line into the container. Using the handle I lowered it over the side until the aperture was below the surface of the sea.

At first the fish viewed it with suspicion, charging up to the entrance then veering off. But they were voracious by nature and seemed determined to outdo each other. Soon two or three fish had gathered at the opening gazing longingly at the lump of bait. Suddenly one of them dashed forward into the container and grabbed the bait and dragged it a little way towards the entrance before backing out. I resisted the temptation to scoop it out and explained to Maurice that we had to

156

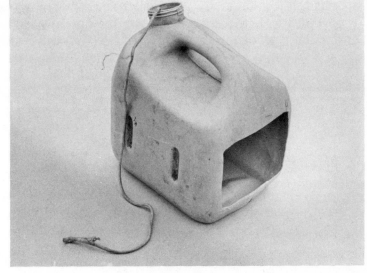

The 'Bailey'
fish-trap
which was used
for the last
half of the
voyage.

get them well trained first. Maurice marvelled at my patience. I fed them lump after lump until a large crowd of fish hung around and willingly played my fish trap game. Eventually, I decided to catch a few and it was so easy to wait for the right fish to swim in and to lift the trap out of the water and deposit the fish at Maurice's feet. The fish didn't appear to notice that some of their playmates had disappeared but continued to oblige with renewed vigour.

Maurice was delighted at the trap's efficiency when I caught our breakfast of approximately twenty fish using very little bait and with no danger of losing our hook. Unfortunately this method of fishing only attracted the trigger fish; the golden jacks and silver fish being much more timid and wary. We could only use the trap in reasonably calm weather. A strong wind would make us drift too fast for the fish to swim into the hole, and a disturbed sea made them misjudge distances. Often they would swim in line with the trap and when they had plucked up sufficient courage, dash forward but because of the movement of the sea they would miss the hole completely. They would then turn round and nuzzle the back of the trap obviously puzzled as to where the bait had gone.

157

Another way we preserved our precious hook was to hold a long piece of steak over the side and wait for the greedy fish to clamp their small but terribly effective teeth on it and quickly flip them into the dinghy. They usually needed a firm tug to dislodge them or a quick bang on the head.

I flipped one into the dinghy and it landed in the bowl of livers and genitals Maurice was preparing for our supper. It ate two of the livers before we could rescue them. Their greediness knew no bounds!

Once I completely stripped a turtle and after much difficulty detached the shoulder bones from the shell. On an impulse I dipped the bone over the side. The fish immediately charged at it. I lifted it out and held it over the dinghy, no fewer than four fish were hanging on to it. Fascinated, I yelled to Maurice to watch and dipped it in again. This time I caught five fish. This was fantastic; nine fish with two dips and no hooks necessary! Exercising great restraint I didn't catch any more but took out the second shoulder bone and kept it ready to fish with the next morning.

"Is it raining?" I asked one day and, after a glance outside, Maurice answered, "No". "Well, what is that noise," I replied. The noise, like the patter of raindrops, was coming closer. I peered out of the vent and soon saw the explanation. A vast shoal of tiny fish was heading towards us running very near to the surface. The sea was pitted with tiny popping bubbles. The shoal seemed to split in two at the raft like an army on parade and joined forces again behind us and continued bubbling on their way. Twice we had found a tiny fish like a herring in the dinghy and assumed the large shoal was of the same kind of fish.

At the beginning of June when, because of Maurice's illness, I had taken over the fishing I had to be extremely careful with the hook as it was the only small one we had left. Maurice always let the fish swallow the hook before he caught them and would use six or eight pieces of bait to catch one fish. This was too slow for me and my expertise had improved so much that, as soon as the fish got close to the bait, I gave the line a jerk. Rather than discourage the fish this had the

158

opposite effect. Once I had jerked it away from them they swam fast towards it and held on tightly to the bait. I would haul them quickly over the side and fling them in the dinghy. My fishing had little style about it but it was fun. Occasionally I got carried away and, jerking the line on board, the fish would whizz through the air attached to the line and land back in the sea on the other side of the dinghy. To me they seemed to enjoy this and there was no lack of contestants for the 'high wire' act.

My fishing sessions became known for the 'flying trigger fish'. As fast as I tossed them in the dinghy Maurice would sort them and throw the smaller ones, 'tadpoles', back over the side. There were so many we could pick and choose. At sessions like this we usually contented ourselves with twenty to thirty fish, but I remember, at least, two occasions when we caught fifty.

Using this method we did not have to keep so much bait on hand as one piece of bait could be used to catch several fish. All we needed was enough bait to catch one fish and then we had fresh bait to start again. It was not unusual to see two fish fly through the air, both hanging on to the same piece of bait.

At other times loud splashes in the distance gradually came closer and closer until we realized the noise was coming from a school of dolphins. Many times we had sat on the foredeck of *Auralyn* as she had ploughed her way across the oceans and watched these graceful creatures gambol alongside us, diving and cavorting in front of the bow. Once, loud squeaking noises had us searching everywhere for the cause only to find we had a school of dolphins alongside talking loudly to each other. Now it seemed these friendly creatures were to visit us once more.

As they came closer we realized they must be catching food and a glance at our shoal of fish cowering in the shade of dinghy and raft made us feel not so well disposed towards them. Suddenly they were amongst us, their black and supple bodies diving in every direction sending the scurrying fish before them. Both rubber craft were tossed about in the

159

Bottle-nosed Dolphin. Approximately eight feet long. It is a small member of the toothed whale family. They usually travel in large schools and are fast, graceful and intelligent.

Dolphins disturbance and dollops of sea water descended on us as they became more and more excited in the chase.

The hullabaloo lasted for almost twenty minutes then suddenly it was still and only an occasional echoing splash in the distance told of their presence. After mopping up and muttering none too complimentary things about them we leaned out and looked at our fish. Only a few bedraggled specimens remained, the rest were dispersed or eaten.

It took many patient hours of feeding and coaxing to get a reasonable sized shoal about us once more and life would again resume its steady routine. The visits of dolphins came to be looked upon as a time of annoyance and frustration and although we aimed at them with our paddles and shouted at them they could not be discouraged. We never managed to hit one, they were far too fast and agile for us, but something had somehow managed to damage them as most of them showed a shattered, chipped or flattened fin.

One morning a plop on the canvas cover turned out to be the one and only squid we saw during our time adrift. It must have been travelling very fast, probably pursued by dolphins or a sperm whale because it hit us with such force. It lay there during the day and by evening the sun had dried it and it had stuck firmly. Squids are related to the octopus and cuttlefish;

160

Sea snakes
and squid

Sea Snake. About twelve to fifteen inches long. They come to the surface to breathe air like all reptiles but swim deep for their food. Brilliantly marked and usually have a dangerous bite. Snakes which spend the whole of their lives at sea produce living young and not eggs.

we didn't feel like eating the creature, it looked like an unappetizing lump of grey jelly. It left a purple ink stain to remind us of its visit.

On several occasions while we sat in the dinghy we had observed sea snakes swimming around. They were deep yellow with black diamond patterns on them. We saw one swimming very close to the surface its head occasionally breaking water, as like all reptiles, it needed to breathe air. I poked it with the paddle and lifted its gleaming body a few inches out of the sea but its supple and sinuous movements made me drop it quickly back into its element. I didn't want a bite from that!

Squid. They are preyed on by toothed whales such as dolphins and sperm whales. They lay eggs on the sea floor, breathe through gills and can swim forwards gently or can project themselves backwards at high speed.

Plankton On many days we saw the sea littered with plankton. Plankton takes its name from the Greek word *plagktos* which means wandering. Some areas are richer in plankton than others and this is partly the reason why whales are prolific in certain areas, since many species of whale and two of the largest fish, the whale shark and the basking shark, feed on plankton. The area in which we were drifting is known to scientists as an intertropical convergence, a region where two ocean currents collide and to be found only north of the equator. Winds blow from the north and the south towards this area resulting in rising air and much rain. The microscopic plankton accumulates along the convergence, thus attracting the various species of fish and other nekton.

One particular piece of plankton caught my eye. It was a lump of transparent jelly about the size of a tomato and with long feelers. As it came undulating closer I picked it up and dropped it into a tin. I stared at this shapeless mass, and although I had read of people eating plankton I tipped the jelly back into the sea and watched it resume its journey. We had not reached that stage yet; we had plenty of fish around us.

Plankton. They propel their bodies through the water using the two whip-like lashes, the flagella.

162

Sucker fish

Sucker Fish (*Remora-Remora*). Approximately twelve inches long. Found all over the world. They attach themselves to the large fish and also marine turtles.

We found the peculiar sucker fish lying in the loose flesh of the turtles' rear flippers. They had attached themselves by means of a large suction disc on top of their heads. It took quite an effort to prise them loose and there was a definite plop as they released their hold. Their pale grey bodies were soft and supple like a snake; they had no scales but a skin of a silky texture and we usually held them in a cloth to stop them slipping about. When one got loose in the dinghy it took a long time to recapture as every time we picked it up it slipped away; it was rather like trying to pick up a tablet of soap in a hot bath. We always found two sucker fish on one reptile, a male and female, each having their separate living quarters, one under each rear flipper.

We used them as bait and the trigger fish adored the rich red meat. If we kept them for an hour or so the flesh turned white. Once we ate them and they had a taste very similar to flying fish.

Brown spine-foots would hover under the raft near the entrance. As they very rarely took the turtle bait I tried to think up another way of catching them. Some kind of spear seemed the best hope. I remembered one of Maurice's navigation instruments, his dividers. I opened them wide and hanging out of the doorway watched for a spine-foot to come within range. When it did I thrust at it with the sharp point.

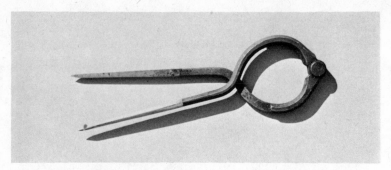

Maurice's navigational dividers that we tried to use as a spear.

The point jarred on its body and I managed to dislodge one scale from its armour plating. I agreed with Maurice that I was more likely to stick it through the raft than through the fish, so reluctantly I gave up the attempt.

June 27th
(115)

One morning as we dozed I was glancing out of the vent, in an effort to maintain a semblance of watch-keeping. I glanced down at the drogue and my attention became riveted by an incredibly large fish hovering lazily behind us. I looked down on to its broad, spotted back and although it seemed shark-like it was too long and broad, at least four feet wide and, possibly, twenty-five to thirty feet long. I sat back in disbelief and explained what I had just seen to Maurice. He got up to investigate and when he saw the creature he agreed it was unlike anything we had previously seen. It hovered between dinghy and raft all morning and we got accustomed to its docile presence and spent a long time watching its graceful motion. By mid-day it had disappeared and we never saw it or its like again. It was not until many months later that we discovered we had been visited by one of Nature's rarest creatures, the largest fish in the world, a whale shark.

Often dawn would reveal heavy grey clouds gathered in an ominous circle around us. Grey streaks from the clouds showed rain falling and more often than not it would come closer and closer, the rain advancing across the water like an army of tiny feet. Then it would sweep over us and race away towards the horizon.

164

Many times these showers came towards us in the opposite direction from the wind. I would ask Maurice if he thought it was going to rain and he would gaze around and answer, "Our weather should be coming from over there and the sky is bright and clear, however, there is a big black cloud over to the left and although it shouldn't, I suppose it will come our way." Usually it did and we became accustomed to receiving our weather from all directions during one day.

Whale Shark. Grows up to forty-five feet long and is the largest fish in the world. It is very rare and was first discovered in 1828, only 100 having been seen since. The one seen by us was approximately twenty-five to thirty feet long. It is very docile and has never been known to attack man.

11 Our World Dissolves at Last

Maralyn

June 30th
(118)

The dawn of June 30th was bright and clear with the promise of a hot day. We tipped some water into the bottom of the dinghy and watched our two baby turtles splash around. We fished for most of the morning and as we scrambled back to the raft for our afternoon siesta, Maurice emptied some more sea water into the dinghy "to keep them cool".

Maurice

For the first time for ages we slept blissfully for longer than one hour. The sun rose higher into a cloudless sky. There was no escape from the aggressive heat and sweat dripped from our naked bodies. The raft bobbed gently in the long ocean swell; there were few waves. At mid-day we ate the remaining fish and complained that it was not very fresh.

We slept again, longer this time. Everything was still, with just a slight southerly breeze roughing the surface of the sea and cooling us through the ventilation hole. How wonderful sleep was.

Maralyn stirred, she was on her knees. Her movements awoke me and I wondered through the fog of sleep what was the matter; perhaps another turtle. I fell asleep again oblivious of Maralyn's effort of pushing her head through the vent.

For a long time I could not rid myself of the feeling that there were three people in the raft, an impression I had frequently had before. In my half-sleep I imagined clearly Maralyn and myself and an American yachtsman called

166

Wayne, whom we had met briefly in Cristobal.

Someone was shaking me, a disembodied voice was calling, "Maurice," and again "Maurice . . ." I thought, "For pity's sake leave me alone and wake Wayne."

"Get out to the dinghy. A ship is coming," Maralyn's urgent tone had penetrated my sluggish brain. Cursing, I automatically struggled to a kneeling position and scrambled across to the dinghy. I sat on the thwart in a dazed condition, trying to focus my eyes on to different parts of the sea. Maralyn was standing in the raft waving her jacket. Yet I could see no ship; Maralyn must be imagining things.

"Wave your jacket, it's there, behind you."

"All right," I said turning round slowly. Then I saw it; a small white, rust-streaked ship approaching from the east. It would pass very close and I began to wave my oilskin jacket. The ship steamed on a course nearly due west and within a short time it was opposite us, about half a mile away.

"It's a Korean fishing boat," I called to Maralyn. "Remember seeing them in Tenerife?"

Maralyn answered but did not stop waving. Her vigorous movements rocked the raft with its nearly deflated lower section almost under water. The ship went past and I stopped waving. It was no use, the ship was not going to stop. Why waste any more energy? I felt ill and slumped to my knees.

I called to Maralyn, "Stop waving, save your strength." She ignored me and continued to wave as the ship showed its stern to us. It was the first we had seen for 43 days.

"Please come back," Maralyn shouted. "Please . . ."

I was oblivious now of the ship's movements as I knelt in the dinghy. Maralyn was still imploring the ship to return. Let it go on, I thought, this is our world now on the sea, amongst the birds and the turtles and the fish.

Maralyn had suddenly stopped her entreaties but continued to wave her jacket quietly. I looked up and stared for some time at the ship. I looked long and hard at it in disbelief. Was it returning or was it a trick of my eyes? Maralyn looked across at me, her eyes moist and gleaming. "It's coming back," she said.

167

168

Maurice

"You've found us a ship," I said excitedly, then realizing our nakedness I went on, "Sort some clothes out, quickly."

She passed over a sodden pair of tennis shorts and a rotting shirt and while we struggled into our clothes, the fishing boat manoeuvred into the wind to come alongside. I reached down and lifted our two young turtles and lowered them over the side.

A heaving line with a heavy 'monkey's fist' on the end descended but it fell short into the sea. Voices shouted from the ship attracting my attention to a second heaving line now draped across the life-raft and the stern of the dinghy. I wedged the monkey's fist hard into the rowlock and strong hands on the ship began to haul our rubber craft towards a boarding ladder up forward.

A voice came down to us, "Can you speak English?"

"We are English," I replied.

Alongside the ladder I secured the dinghy with another line and, holding on to the ladder, I began to haul the raft close so that Maralyn could go on board first. A seaman jumped down and stood beside me and indicated that I should board first. "Go on, I'll follow," Maralyn said. I climbed the ladder and over the bulwarks to be greeted by a number of willing arms to support me. I was led across to a blanket laid on deck, but because of my sores, I could not sit. I half knelt taking most of my weight on my arms and thighs.

On previous
page
Maurice grabs the end of the heaving line which is draped across the canopy of the raft and fixes the end into the rowlock of the dinghy. Maralyn, at this time, is putting some clothes on inside the raft.

170

A seaman from the *Weolmi* holds the ladder whilst Maurice prepares to clamber aboard.

Maralyn

June 30th
at 4 p.m. Within minutes I too was pulled alongside and another sailor held the raft close to the ladder as I climbed towards the deck.

I was helped over the bulwarks and when they let go of me I sank to my knees. I thought it was the heaving and rolling of the deck but when I tried to stand again I realized it was my legs and not the ship. After four months of sitting my legs refused to take the weight of my body. I looked round for Maurice and saw him sitting on a blanket several feet away. I indicated I wanted to join him and soon I was installed on the blanket next to him.

I remembered the many Korean fishing boats we had seen in the small fishing harbour at Tenerife. Several of the seamen had helped us then to lower the groceries into the dinghy as we loaded up *Auralyn* for her trans-Atlantic crossing. We never expected to meet up with any of them again, but how glad I was that we had.

A beaming cook approached us with two glasses of hot, steaming milk. All around us were happy smiling faces and I found it hard to hold back the tears of joy as, between sips of milk, I tried to express my thanks.

We looked at each other and for the moment we were unaware of the men crowding around us. Maurice said, "We've made it," and I replied: "Now for *Auralyn II*—and Patagonia!"

Right A seaman helps Maralyn as she climbs the ladder, whilst other willing hands reach down to haul her aboard.

172

173

Maurice

June 30th
1973
The ship's powerful 8-cylinder diesel engine was once more throbbing away and she turned on to her course as we were helped into a cabin in the officers' quarters.

The ship, *Weolmi 306*, we learned was a tuna fishing boat of 650 tons out of Busan, and was on its way home to South Korea after some thirty months fishing in the Atlantic Ocean. She had been based at Las Palmas in the Canary Islands and would hunt for tuna for up to six months at a time. She would then return to Las Palmas to land her catch for canning.

Suh Jung Il, the captain, sat at the table in our cabin writing down our answers to his many questions. He was amazed at our story and interrogated us at length.

"Are you sure you are not Russian?" Mr. Suh asked. (In Korea, we discovered, the family name always follows the title of address and then the given names.) Perhaps my growth of beard had aroused his suspicions. Even the production of our British passports, which we had saved, did not convince him. "If you are Russian—big trouble," he said in broken English. It was perhaps half an hour before we could convince him that we did not belong to a state with communist affiliations.

"We will help you," Mr. Suh said. "But crew very tired and want to return to Korea quickly."

Very thankful for our rescue, I replied "If you would take us to Korea, we are happy."

"I will radio my company in Seoul and tell them about you," he said. "And if you wish me to, I send message to your agents in England."

"Thank you," I said slowly, "I would like to commend your lookout for spotting us. It was a very good effort." I had difficulty in making myself understood as my north-country English was so different from the American English the captain was used to. Mr. Suh found that he could understand Maralyn more easily and he began to address his questions to her. I was pleased to let Maralyn handle the rest of the interrogation.

174

On board
Weolmi

The strain shows in our faces as we gratefully eat one of our first meals on board.

"We will help you," the captain repeated. "We give you clothes and food." He then indicated my sores. "Every day my engineer come and give you medicine."

I looked around at the sea of faces in that small cabin and, unable to disguise my happiness, I smiled at each one, regretting my inability to show our gratitude more effectively. Crew members would pass the door and, unable to speak English, were content to stand and smile at us. A feeling of well-being enveloped us; we had goodwill for everyone.

The questioning was brought to an abrupt conclusion with the appearance of Jun Sang Won, the cook, with a tray of food for us.

"Only little at a time now," Mr. Jun said. "Afterwards more." He spoke English well. We were left alone to enjoy out meal of two fried eggs, a bowl of vegetable soup, bread and butter and two large glasses of hot sweetened milk.

Bai Seok Dong, the chief engineer, came to the cabin later to dress my sores. He had served, he told us, in the medical

175

corps of the South Korean army. Patiently and expertly Mr.
Bai cleaned and dressed my wounds.

"I have excused Kim Young Gon all watchkeeping duties
in the engine room so that he can look after you couple,"
Mr. Bai told us. "He wash your clothes and fetch water and
clean cabin." Again we tried to convey our thanks, but Mr.
Bai shrugged and went on, "I must ask you please to take
these vitamin pills and these tetramycin tablets." He handed
me a bottle of vitamin pills and one antibiotic tablet each. "I
will bring these tablets each day," Mr. Bai said.

Mr. Kim Young Gon would fuss over us, attending to all
our needs and helping us in every way possible. Mr. Bai came
every day and dressed my sores and brought the tetramycin
tablets. We slept for much of each day, waking sometimes
only when Mr. Jun came with our next meal. Movement was
very painful for us and we could do little but hobble about
the deck supporting ourselves on the ship's guardrails. We
would climb to the bridge before dawn each day to watch the
sun rise, amazed at our good fortune at being able to walk
about on the solid security of a ship again.

Our skeleton-thin frames began to fill out, but our joints
remained painfully stiff and our legs and feet became swollen
after some exercise due, we discovered, to protein deficiency.
Mr. Bai shaved my beard off and Maralyn was shocked to
see my spare features. We were sure life would return to
normal only after several months of recuperation.

Every day we would rest in our cabin waving a greeting to
members of the crew as they passed by. Many would stop to
drop gifts on to our table. Toothpaste, clothes, soap, toothbrushes, chocolate, biscuits and cosmetics for Maralyn. Some
of these were presents intended for their families in Korea.
The bosun made a gift of his only belts to hold up our
trousers, whilst he improvised with a necktie for his own.

The captain and crew volunteered to forgo the luxuries of
chicken, beef, water melon, pineapple, milk, eggs and bread
so that there would be ample 'European' food for us. They also
gave us tuna which they had been keeping as gifts for their
families.

The raft and dinghy are put proudly inflated on the deck with all the equipment so that we can pose with the captain and most of his crew.

All this generosity moved us deeply and, as our voyage continued, we began to feel as though we belonged to that ship. We were shown kindness and courtesy in everything; the crew could not do enough for us and our affection for them grew. We really wanted to be part of that crew.

Song Jong Soo, the first officer, lent us magazines and Yoon Young Soo lent us his books printed, surprisingly in English. Everyone who could speak our tongue wanted to talk to us glad of the opportunity to improve their English.

"English spoken by American GI's no good," they would say. I wondered often if our north-country accents ever disillusioned them.

After a few days the captain's message to his company
had been received in Seoul and, if the resulting avalanche of
telegrams were any guide, it must have caused some excitement there. Messages came to the Captain from many
countries through Korean radio stations. Mr. Suh passed on
to us messages of congratulations from our friends and from
newspapers looking for a story. The radio officer, Bok Jin
Woon, worked long hours to deal with incoming messages
and their replies. He sometimes conscientiously maintained
a radio watch during his periods of rest.

At first we could not condition ourselves to the overwhelm-
ing interest shown in our ordeal by people from all over the
world. We were now looking for a solution to our problems,
and were content with the mundane task of planning our
future and of working to provide ourselves with money for
another boat.

"Mr. and Mrs. Bailey couple," Mr. Suh announced one
day, a sheaf of telegrams in his hand. "You are world
sensation."

Even then we did not believe that sitting in a raft for 117
days could cause a sensation. He must be exaggerating we
thought. Still the telegrams poured in; it became impossible
for us to answer them all. Everyone wanted our story.

"The world people wait to have news," said Mr. Suh. "And
all Korean people wish meet you when we reach Busan. They
all wish your health and good fortune."

This first made us realize that our ordeal was not merely a
momentary non-event ready-made for the mass-media, but
people were genuinely interested. *In us!* It was unbelievable
that our simple undertaking would ultimately receive such
public acclaim.

"All Korean people impatient. They want to welcome you
in Korea," Mr. Suh said carefully. "We shall sail into Busan in
Weolmi together."

Unfortunately the Captain's plan failed to materialize
because his company, due to doubts about the condition of
our health, instructed him to put into Honolulu for us to receive medical treatment.

178

Friday
July 13th   This we know caused a lot of disappointment to the Captain and his crew as we had promised to spend time with them and to meet their families in Busan. They sadly thought that once we had landed at Honolulu and tasted the comforts of American living we would not wish to travel to Korea. We tried to reassure them that it was our wish to continue on board *Weolmi* to Korea, but we felt that they were unconvinced.

During the morning of Friday, July 13th the island of Oahu hove in sight and little did we imagine the excitement we had caused.

Within a short time the ship had docked in Honolulu amidst a tumultuous reception with a typical Hawaiian

Weolmi from the air, approaching Honolulu.

179

With the captain between us, we shakily walk down the gangway led by the Korean ambassador.

welcome of leis and kisses. Newspapermen and television reporters crowded around us with their many questions unanswered due to the crush. Once more Captain Suh came to our rescue and we were ushered away and taken into the city by the Koreans who bought more clothes for us.

Our medical examination took only a few days and we stayed at the Sheraton Waikiki hotel as guests of the management. The Captain and his crew meanwhile waited patiently for us. *Weolmi*'s owners, after much consideration, decided that they could not permit us to travel by their ship, because, being only a fishing boat, it did not possess adequate medical facilities. The disappointment to us was considerable; we longed to be aboard and to share once more in the life of that ship.

As the ship left the dockside we waved sadly shouting "Annyonghi Kesipsiyo", "Ch'ukpok hapnida" (goodbye and good luck) to the crew and we made a vow that we would meet them all again when *Weolmi* arrived in Korea. Nothing would stop us.

180

The end of
the ordeal

Maralyn

Our days on the ship amongst these fun-loving people had been a time of suspension—a limbo between our life of solitude and the maelstrom of civilization which awaited us in Honolulu and beyond. It was a happy time, a time to renew human relationships, a time of recovery, of hope, of planning. In the words of the song "a time to be sowing, a time to be reaping . . ." We had sowed and reaped, and our harvest of knowledge was a bountiful one.

Appendices

i The Life-Raft

by Maralyn Bailey

Our life-raft was a four-man size made by the Avon
Rubber Co. It was only 4′ 6″ in internal diameter, therefore
it was impossible to stretch our limbs fully. We would have
had to have taken an eight-man raft to have achieved this
luxury.

Basically, the raft was sound and we only found minor
irritations, some of which have already been rectified by the
makers. The *velcro* 'door' fastening became ineffective and
the slightest breeze would whip the door open. The press-
studs were too small and popped open at the slightest
pressure. We think we would have been better served with
heavy duty press-studs and a plastic zip.

We only managed to fasten the sea-anchor to the back of
the raft because I was small and could wriggle my head and
shoulders through the ventilator. Apparently the sea-anchor
is usually fastened to the front, but this means the doorway
faces the oncoming waves, not a desirable position. If the
vent was slightly larger to enable a man to reach the outside
tube, with a fixing point provided, the sea-anchor could be
placed in the correct position.

The raft was four years old and had been sent away for
regular servicing. It was last serviced one month before we
left England. It was inflated only eleven months later yet
certain things were not in order, e.g. the light would not
work as the battery was broken: there was no instruction
card: the glue in the repair kit had perished and hardened:
the CO_2 cylinder escaped from its fastenings on inflation
and hung free. Fortunately this had no effect on the

inflation but caused us many anxious moments as the drogue line was constantly being fouled by it.

The repair kit consisted of two-part glue, patches and a pair of ordinary steel scissors. The process involved in using two-part glues is lengthy and impossible to apply in certain conditions in a small craft. Some form of self-adhesive tape would have been more realistic. It was also fortunate that we had a pair of stainless steel scissors, as the ones provided rusted solid in a very short time.

There was only one reinforced fixing point for a rope, and this was wrenched out in a storm. Most people, if they had time, would try and take a dinghy with them when abandoning a yacht, therefore two reinforced points would be valuable.

The bright orange cover soon lost its colour and, therefore was no longer of any use as an aid to rescue; it would not have attracted the necessary attention. It also lost its waterproofing properties very quickly. If the top could incorporate some form of radar reflector it might prove

The raft pump, showing the emergency repairs made by Maralyn using medical adhesive plaster.

183

useful. Nowadays keeping watch on board some vessels, especially in mid-ocean, merely entails watching a radar screen.

The sea-anchor was not very substantial and had no swivel fitting, therefore it twisted round and round until the hemp rope unlaid and finally broke.

The pump, igloo shaped, began to split round the base. We held it together by the judicious use of first-aid plasters. Even then air escaped each time it was used and made the job of pumping the raft twice as long and exhausting.

The Dinghy

This was also made by Avon, a nine foot long Redcrest model. We had bought it in 1969 and it was serviced with the life-raft just before we began our voyage.

It never gave us any problems and withstood an incredible amount of hard wear and tear. We often feared a puncture from fish spines, sharks, or from dragging turtles around inside it, but it appeared indestructible. We would both hang over on one side and drag a 200 pound turtle on board yet we never had the slightest qualm about its stability. It did overturn three times, but this was in storm conditions and probably because its movements were restricted by the raft.

184

ii Acknowledgements

We wish to take this opportunity of expressing our deep gratitude to all those people who have assisted us since our rescue.

In Honolulu our thanks are extended to Professor and Mrs. Folsom (Clair and Jo) for their wonderful hospitality; to Mr. Simon Cardew and the management of the Sheraton Waikiki Hotel; to Mr. Barr, the British Consul-General and Mrs. Barr; to Mr. Brunt the British Vice-Consul; to Dr. and Mrs. McKenzie-Pollock; to Dr. Millard; to Dr. Tashima and Dr. Tabral, both of Hawaii University Medical School; to Dr. and Mrs. Sun Woo Nam; to Mr. Lee, the Korean Ambassador, and his efficient staff.

During our visit to South Korea we had the good fortune to meet many people who showed us extreme warm-hearted kindness and courtesy. To all those people we wish to proffer our sincere and heart-felt thanks. In particular, Mr. Sang Man Kim, president of Dong-A Ilbo, our host; to his staff especially Mr. Kwon Sang Park and Mr. Hung Won Park; to Mr. Hwan Eui Lee, president of the Mun.. Hwa Radio and TV Co. and his staff: to Mr. Taek Shik Yang, Mayor of Seoul, for the splendid gift of honorary citizenship of Seoul; to Mr. Kim Jung Hwan of the Korea Tourist Bureau; Mr. K. U. Chee of the Hyundai Construction Co.; to Mr. Kap-Chong Chi; to Professor S. H. P. Cheung of the U.S.A.; to Dr. Okja Choi Choo of the Sejong Hotel, Seoul; Mr. Kin Je Tu of the Kuk Dong Hotel, Busan; to Mr. Peterson, the British Ambassador and Mrs. Peterson; to Mr. S. E. Wang,

Acknowledge-
ments
British Vice-Consul in Busan; to Colonel Stewart of the
U.S. army and his command at Panmunjon; to the Korean
army for the escort they provided for our visit to Gloucester
Valley.

There are many, many others whom we should like to
reiterate our thanks for making our visit to South Korea so
memorable. We shall not forget any of them.

A special thank you must go to Mr. and Mrs. Ivor Davis
of Los Angeles who willingly smoothed our paths for so
long. Also to Mr. and Mrs. Colin Foskett of Southampton.

It is perhaps fitting to mention at this point our
indebtedness to the management of the Korean Marine
Industries Development Corporation whose initial
thoughtful care made it possible for us to regain our health
so quickly.

We are extremely grateful to Commander and Mrs. Erroll
Bruce for inviting us to share their home at Lymington
during our first few weeks in England. Mr. and Mrs.
Adlard Coles and Major and Mrs. Bill Martineau earned our
lasting gratitude for placing their respective charming
houses at our disposal whilst we wrote this book. Our
sincere thanks are accorded to Daphne Bruce who kindly
read the manuscript and made many valuable comments.

We are indebted to Mr. Reg Tayler, Mr. Dan Bowen and
Mr. Alan Moody for organizing a fund to help us on our
return to England.

We are equally indebted for the help we received from
Mrs. Elizabeth Rowell, Mrs. Hilda Devonshire and
Miss Caroline Hodsoll and the other staff of Nautical
Publishing Company who have patiently deciphered our
sometimes illegible manuscript and typed the copy for the
printer.

To all these people we humbly dedicate our book.

iii Medical Aspects of Survival

By Surgeon Captain John Duncan Walters, M.B., B.S.,
M.F.C.M., D.I.H., D.P.H., Royal Navy of the
Institute of Naval Medicine

Given a thermal environment in which the body can maintain its normal temperature and a sufficiency of fresh water, shortage of food can be tolerated for a considerable period before obvious signs of starvation appear, although such deprivation adversely affects morale. Energy requirements vary widely according to circumstances as well as between individuals but, taking the adult population as a whole, the average male requires more energy input and has smaller reserves in the form of fat than the female. It follows, therefore, that the female of the species should fare better in the face of starvation and this would appear to be true since Maralyn was in much better physical condition at the end of the voyage than was Maurice.

Under famine conditions it is unusual for protein foods to be the most plentiful. The Bailey's, however, were deriving from the sea a diet composed almost entirely of protein, plus a little fat, although this fat was in relatively small and irregular supply. It was, therefore, very fortunate that they were able to catch sufficient rain water to enable this protein to be digested, absorbed into the body and its waste products eliminated. Protein digestion and the elimination of the inevitable waste products is costly in terms of water requirements, whilst sugar is not demanding in this respect. For this reason, amongst others, it is usual to include sugar in survival packs rather than protein foods.

Trigger fish and turtles provided the bulk of their food. It has often been stated that the trigger fish is poisonous and should not, therefore, be eaten. It appears, however, that it

187

may be safe to eat when caught in the open sea but, when they are close inshore feeding upon a particular type of coral, they become poisonous. Another interesting fact about fish, which may be of significance in the Bailey's case since they showed few signs of scurvy when rescued, is that the relatively small amount of vitamin C in fish is concentrated mainly in the eyes, brain and pancreas, all of which they consumed with relish.

The turtles provided a large quantity of protein, some glandular tissues such as liver, kidney and spleen, and a considerable quantity of blood. Green turtles are the most common in the area where the raft drifted and it has been reported that this particular species has a hypotonic blood plasma, so that it would be useful, in the survival situation, to drink the blood. The protein content of turtle meat compares very well with that of other protein foods, being slightly less than raw beef steak and somewhat more than raw white fish. Unlike beef steak, however, which contains about 10% fat, turtle meat contains only $\frac{1}{2}\%$. Since fat is a very concentrated form of energy which can provide over twice as much energy for a given weight than either protein or carbohydrate, turtle meat would not, for a given quantity, provide as much available energy as would raw steak.

The problem about living on the type of diet upon which the Bailey's subsisted was, therefore, that they would be obliged to consume a very large quantity of the food available to meet the energy demands of their bodies even before any was utilized for the repair and replacement of their tissues. That their food intake was insufficient to provide for these requirements is clear from the fact that they both lost about forty pounds weight during their ordeal. Quite early in their survival period Maralyn noted that their ribs were showing and that other bones protruded sharply indicating that there was a rapid reduction in their fat reserves.

Both of them suffered from salt water boils which, in Maurice's case, later broke down and coalesced in the region of the sacrum and buttocks to form deep and painful ulcers which persisted throughout the voyage but healed soon after their rescue. Maralyn had no menstrual periods for three months after the first which was ten days late, but it is not uncommon for women to suffer upsets in the menstrual cycle in times of stress from whatever cause. Taking these together with all the other signs, however, a picture of a progressive dietary deficiency state can be seen to be developing.

It is known that both Maralyn and Maurice were anaemic when they were rescued, although the degree of this anaemia is not known. Some three weeks later, however, their haemoglobin levels were 11.9 and 11.4 grams per 100 millilitres blood respectively. These figures show that a degree of anaemia was present in both cases, probably due to a combination of factors since anaemia is common in a number of deficiency states, and also that Maurice was slightly more anaemic than Maralyn. Under normal circumstances the average male has more haemoglobin per unit volume of blood than the average female of the human species, so that the reversal of the position in this case is further evidence that Maurice suffered more from his privations than did his wife.

After rescue, both survivors suffered from swollen limbs and reported tenderness of the shin bones especially and pain and stiffness in the joints. The anaemia already noted and the pain in the limbs could be explained on the basis of a deficiency of certain vitamins, particularly vitamins B and C, but investigations, at present incomplete, may shed more light on this point. Likewise, these further investigations may provide an explanation for the chest pain, associated with coughing up blood, which affected Maurice. His condition may have been associated with the breaking down of an old scar resulting from an earlier chest infection but another possibility is that the pain in his legs was due, at least in part, to some thrombosis in the veins which gave rise to small blood clots which were deposited in the lungs by way of the blood stream.

Why Maralyn's finger nails lost their natural coloration is an interesting problem. The normal translucent pinkish colour of the finger nails was maintained for the first month in the raft and then, over a period of about two weeks, they changed from pink to pale pink and, finally, pearly white.

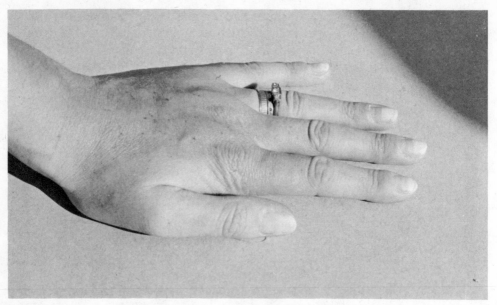

Taken two months after rescue, Maralyn's fingers still show the white discoloration which has, at this time, worked its way about half way down her nails.

They did not become unnaturally brittle or deformed, and, now the nails are growing out, a distinct transverse line of demarcation between pearly white and the normal colour may be seen on each nail. Although the feet were equally exposed to the elements the toe nails did not show the same discoloration, and, whilst various suggestions and explanations for the phenomenon have been offered, no final conclusions have yet been reached.

Evidence regarding the mental and emotional state of Maralyn and Maurice during and immediately following their voyage is difficult to evaluate in retrospect but it does not seem that they have suffered any permanent incapacity in this regard. The difficulties arise not only because of the lack of objective evidence but also because mental deterioration can occur in association with dietary deficiencies as well as with prolonged isolation in a hostile environment. Nevertheless, the story as it has been told shows that it is possible to survive

190

in the face of apparently insurmountable odds without irreversible mental deterioration.

At the time of the sinking both Maralyn and Maurice were sufficiently calm for them to stock the raft with a very sensible assortment of water, food and oddments which were subsequently to prove immensely valuable. This confidence at a time of great stress derives largely from good training in survival techniques and confidence in one's knowledge so that panic, with its possibly fatal results, is minimized. Under the stimulus of such danger the body reacts with an increase in physical and mental activity which subsequently gives way to a period of adaptation to the survival situation. If the survival period is prolonged there will be a degree of mental deterioration dependant upon individual reaction and to physical circumstances. Irritability, aggressiveness, selfishness and daydreaming are common. Especially when water and food are in short supply there appears a preoccupation with drink and food. Sometimes suicidal or homicidal tendencies occur or delirium but frank madness is unusual unless the castaway has been drinking sea water or is suffering from severe wounds or illness.

In the case of Maralyn and Maurice there were periods of depression, anxiety, tenseness and self-reproach but they overcame these difficulties extremely well. They fished, played games with improvised equipment, wrote a great deal and discussed the future, all of which activities must have assisted in maintaining morale and thus their chances of survival. The value of their will to survive is obvious from their story and, without this will, it is doubtful if they would have survived even had they possessed more sophisticated aids than were actually available.

Having briefly reviewed some of the medical aspects of Maralyn and Maurice's survival against apparently impossible odds, it should be pointed out that the story is far from complete. It is important, however, that the investigations should be carried through to completion so that the experience gained may be used for the possible benefit of others placed in a similarly unfortunate position.

iv Summary of Ship Sightings

1st Ship   March 12 (Day 8) At 0800 hrs. Heading East. Distance 1 mile. Let off flares (4). Waved. Sea calm.

2nd Ship   March 29 (Day 25) At 0400 hrs. Heading South. Distance $\frac{1}{2}$ mile. Let off flares. Sea calm.

3rd Ship   April 10 (Day 37) At 1000 hrs. Heading East. Distance 1 mile. Waved, made smoke. Sea rough.

4th Ship   April 12 (Day 39) At 1530 hrs. Heading South. Distance $\frac{1}{2}$ mile. Waved. Sea rough. Ship stopped made two 180° turns. Did not come closer. Went on.

5th Ship   April 18 (Day 45) At midnight. Heading West. Distance $1\frac{1}{2}$ miles. Sea moderate. Kerosene flares unsuccessful, torch.

6th Ship   May 8 (Day 65) At 1830 hrs. Heading East. Distance 1 mile. Sea calm. Waved.

7th Ship   May 18 (Day 75) At 1145 hrs. Heading East. Distance $1\frac{1}{2}$ miles. Sea calm. Waved.

8th Ship   June 30th (Day 118) At 1600 hrs. Heading West. Distance $\frac{1}{2}$ mile. Sea calm. Waved. Ship stopped. Korean fishing boat—*Weolmi 306*